Assessment for Learning without Limits

Assessment for Learning without Limits

Alison Peacock

Open University Press

Open University Press
McGraw-Hill Education
8th Floor
338 Euston Road
London
NW1 3BH

email: enquiries@openup.co.uk
world wide web: www.openup.co.uk

and Two Penn Plaza, New York, NY 10121-2289, USA

First published 2016

Front cover design by nursery children from The Wroxham School in the style of Yvonne Coomber.

A catalogue record of this book is available from the British Library

ISBN-13: 978-0-33-526136-9
ISBN-10: 0-33-526136-1
eISBN: 978-0-33-526137-6

Library of Congress Cataloging-in-Publication Data
CIP data applied for

Typeset by Aptara, Inc.

Printed and bound by CPI Group (UK) Ltd, Croydon, CR0 4YY

Praise for this book

"Alison Peacock is a treasure. She has remarkable wisdom about the purposes of education and the processes that make education work. In this book, she shares that wisdom, showing how judicious assessments can awaken students' motivation to learn and create eager, effective learners. Everyone who cares about children's lives and their futures should read this book!"

Carol S. Dweck, Professor of Psychology, Stanford University,
US and author of Mindset

"This book is brimming with practical solutions and high quality strategies to help teachers assess progress in partnership with their pupils. It serves as a timely reminder that children's ability is far from fixed – as all the education evidence demonstrates. By synthesising an array of evidence, this book offers an enlightened approach to assessments that works for children, educators and parents alike."

Lee Elliot Major, Chief Executive of the Sutton Trust and
co-author of the Sutton Trust-EEF toolkit for teachers

"Any teacher or leader feeling ground-down or disenfranchised needs to read this book. Its agenda and commitment are uplifting - to generate a love of learning and realise achievement in every child, irrespective of their circumstances or prior attainment. Assessment for Learning Without Limits rejects the ability labels which are so often linked to social class trends and segregation in our schools. A commitment to high expectations and social justice permeates the book, yet Alison Peacock's method is to encourage and excite teachers, rather than hammering and bureaucratizing. Her arguments are inspiring and convincing, supported by lively case studies and research evidence."

Professor Becky Francis, Director, UCL Institute of Education, UK

"This book tackles the difficult and very important task of bringing together the Learning Without Limits big ideas and the challenging topic of assessment. In it, Alison Peacock shows clearly the damage done by assessment contaminated by ability-labelling and other ability-based practices, and argues the moral and educational necessity of doing assessment in a different way.

Distinctive features of the book include a sustained emphasis on the necessary conditions for transformability, a key concept in the original Learning without Limits study. Another is the argument for the centrality of formative assessment – assessment that works for children, and every aspect of their learning. Drawing on her experience as headteacher, with contributions from other primary and secondary school staff groups across the country, Alison Peacock makes a powerful case for trust and dialogue as the essential building blocks of this 'different way'."

Mary Jane Drummond and Susan Hart, Co-authors of Learning without
Limits and Creating Learning without Limits, UK

"This is a great book, and as one of the nine teachers who was part of the original 'Learning without Limits' research project I can vouch for Dame Alison Peacock's unswerving commitment to, and passion for, the principles of Learning without Limits embodied within its pages. Throughout the book, powerful and authentic stories about leading, learning, listening, dialogue and trust bring a bold and transformative approach to assessment within the grasp of all educational practitioners and leaders.

However, this is not just a book about assessment, but a book about leadership through partnership, founded upon the principles of Learning without Limits. The ten key leadership practices for building trust, outlined at the start of the book, are vital for success across the whole educational sector and should be taken to heart by all those involved in teaching and learning, whether it be at primary, secondary, further or higher education level."

Dr Claire Taylor, Deputy Vice-Chancellor,
Wrexham Glyndŵr University, UK

"In contrast to some rather 'dry' books on assessment that start with abstract principles and seek illustrations of them, this book works the other way around. It is full of rich stories of practice and the voices of children and their teachers. In this way the integral connections among assessment, pedagogy and curriculum are made very clear. The vital importance of listening to children, engaging in dialogue for

understanding, and communication with parents and carers, in an atmosphere of trust, is emphasised. Yet, teachers and leaders will be reassured that assessment for learning, as distinct from assessment purely for accountability can lead to excellent performance without any need for 'ability labelling' of children."

Mary James, Professor Emerita, University of Cambridge
Faculty of Education, UK

Dedication

I should like to dedicate this book to my wonderful family who have truly inspired me to maintain the professional courage needed to always put children first.
Sadly, Michael Armstrong, co-author of Chapter Five, died before this book was published. I shall always be grateful to him for his personal support and generosity in sharing his brilliant analysis of children's writing.

Alison Peacock

Contents

Acknowledgements		x
Introduction		1
1	Building a professional learning culture of trust	4
2	Learning to listen: Finding a way through for every child	18
3	A language for thinking: Assessment through dialogue	34
4	Beyond differentiation: Avoiding labelling	51
5	Assessing writing	65
6	Reporting to families: Sharing assessment without levels or grades	83
7	A whole-school approach to assessment	99
8	Principled innovative leadership for transformability	116
Bibliography		133
Index		136

Acknowledgements

With grateful thanks to the children and teachers from the following schools:

Banstead Infant School, Surrey
Beaudesert Lower School, Leighton Buzzard
Bridgewater Primary School, Northampton
Cherry Orchard Primary School, Worcester
College Park Infant School, Portsmouth
East Barnet School, London
Eaton Primary, Norfolk
Greenfield Academy, Bristol
Larkrise Primary School, Oxfordshire
Meredith Infant School, Portsmouth
Morpeth School, London
Moss Hey Primary School, Stockport
Nishkam High School, Birmingham
Park Street C of E Primary School, St Albans
Rosendale Primary School, London
Scole CE VC Primary, Norfolk
St Helen's Primary School, Ipswich
St Mary's C of E Primary School, Barnet
St Nicolas C of E School, Berkshire
Sunnyfields Primary School, Barnet
The University of Cambridge Primary School
The Wroxham School, Hertfordshire

Thanks also to Dr Paul Browning, Queensland, Australia,
Professor Michael Armstrong, Mike Ollerton, Vanessa Pearce and
Norman Thomas.

Introduction

Building on the success of *Learning without Limits* (Hart et al. 2004) and *Creating Learning without Limits* (Swann et al. 2012), this book explores what happens when teachers and school leaders have the professional courage to adopt principles and practices of *Learning without Limits* that reject notions of fixed intelligence and ability labelling. The original *Learning without Limits* study found that three core principles are at the heart of pedagogy that does not limit children. These principles are *trust*, *co-agency* and the *ethic of everybody*. It is these principles that matter when trying to adopt classroom and leadership practices that remove the determinism associated with ability labelling. In *Creating Learning without Limits* the study moved forwards to focus on creating an alternative approach to school development across a whole school, The Wroxham School (where I was the newly appointed headteacher), similarly pursuing the principles of *Learning without Limits* and thus underpinned by a flourishing of expertise and hope, as opposed to deficit and blame.

In this book, I explore further what can be achieved when we remove limits on learning in primary, secondary and special schools through a rich range of examples, anecdotes and practical hands-on experience, which have been welcomed from a wide variety of sources. At education conferences all over the country I have been approached by colleagues, often diffident at first, but keen to share the story of work developing in their classroom or across their school. These are stories of hope about an alternative approach to learning and assessment that enables children to experience learning far beyond their own and others' expectations. At a time of increasing pressure on school results, tracking of progress and a persistent view that children's future attainment can, and should, be mapped and micro-measured from their earliest days, here we discover ways of fanning the flames of the 'learning without limits' ethic to enable transformative change for schools, for teachers and most importantly, for children.

In tandem with the growing recognition of the power of *Learning without Limits*, Carol Dweck's influence is also increasingly being felt in schools that are keen to promote her ideas about a growth mindset (2012). At a time when schools all over England are in pursuit of new assessment practices and reporting of progress since National Curriculum levels were abandoned by the government in 2014, the insights throughout this book about what is possible are ever more pertinent.

What is wrong with the idea of so-called 'ability'?

For too long we have unquestioningly accepted the idea that learning is easily measurable through tests, that 'progress' can easily be defined and that intelligence is fixed. The problem with words such as 'ability', 'progress' and 'potential' is that they convey an assumption that every child has a pre-programmed, fixed and limited capacity to learn. If learning is assumed to be like a ladder, it follows that schools should be held accountable and blamed if children do not attain test scores that fit this pattern. This has led to a culture in many schools that has become dominated by performance, as displayed for public scrutiny via 'data dashboards' and league tables. If children are not making the expected progress relative to their peers, particularly in English and mathematics, there is an assumption that it is the teacher's responsibility to force the child to the next rung on the ladder. The pressure for improved performance is felt not only by the child, but also by their parents, their teacher, their school and their local authority. Too often, high stakes testing has led to pressure for measurable performance at the expense of learning.

The art of good teaching is to enable each learner to practise skills, debate ideas, make connections and gain knowledge within a meaningful context. This is best achieved within a climate of trust where 'personal best' is sought, rather than ranking or point-scoring. Assessment in such classrooms will be enhanced by a rich and varied curriculum, taught by colleagues with good subject knowledge and pedagogical expertise. The richer and more open-ended the curriculum is, the greater the opportunity for the teacher to assess understanding and misconceptions. The quality of teaching and breadth of curriculum experience are vital. Too often, learning can be overly dominated by tests and exams to the extent that students in many secondary classrooms are intolerant of any activity that does not have a direct link to what may be expected of them within a forthcoming test. The key is to create a learning environment where assessment is understood as a lifelong process of self-improvement and ambition, in the broadest sense.

International concern

There is increasing interest both nationally and internationally in alternative approaches to pedagogy that reject deterministic notions of fixed intelligence. The principles of *Learning without Limits* and the ideas of *Creating Learning without Limits* have been noted across the world from Spain to Australia, New Zealand, Japan, Thailand and the USA. The value and impact of listening to children makes sense to those seeking hope for a better future in education.

An alternative to ability grouping

For well over a decade now at The Wroxham School, we have offered a system of choice and challenge within lessons that may previously have been differentiated by the teacher. This approach is probably one of the most popular aspects of our school as far as the children are concerned. When we had an inspection in 2009, the lead inspector was almost literally bowled over by children rushing to tell him about the opportunities they were given to challenge themselves in their learning. Refusing to set limits on children's learning by labelling them according to preconceived assumptions about what they may achieve enables a culture of co-agency to flourish. Throughout this book we explore this 'challenge' approach further and discover the practical ways in which teachers in many schools are engaging in assessment in partnership with children.

What follows is a focus initially on the core areas of leadership that enable a culture of opportunity, thereby offering a rich resource to assess learning. We encounter vision and transformative leadership, curriculum creativity, structures that enable voices to be heard, whole-school assessment systems and specific assessment techniques in relation to the analysis of writing. Many examples are drawn from practice at The Wroxham School, together with a large number of examples drawn from other primary and secondary schools where an inclusive culture of opportunity flourishes. Every one of these stories inspires hope that school improvement and individual achievement can be reached through an alternative agenda of collective empowerment and ambition. Throughout the book you will witness the liberating power of trust, co-agency and inclusion; as opposed to targets, tracking and fear.

Every September our Year Six teacher reads the poem 'Come to the Edge' by Christopher Logue (1969) to her class. She tells them that they will be given every opportunity to challenge themselves, to surprise themselves and to achieve more than anyone knew they could. Children throughout the school find this pedagogy remarkably liberating.

I urge you, too, to 'Come to the edge', engage with these stories, build professional courage . . . and never look back.

1
Building a professional learning culture of trust

If you don't have the trust of your staff you will have no followers, you will be an emancipated leader – going places, but on your own.

(Paul Browning, Principal, Queensland, Australia)

Pedagogy, curriculum and assessment are the core areas of expertise that form the foundations for all good teaching. This book builds on the research studies *Learning without Limits* (Hart et al. 2004) and *Creating Learning without Limits* (Swann et al. 2012) that offer an alternative pedagogy, inspired by a relentless focus on *every* child's capacity to learn. The first study researched the classrooms of nine primary and secondary teachers, of whom I was one. Each of us was working in a way that sought to swim against the tide of target-setting that reduced the complexity of learners to numbers or grades. The second study focused on an alternative approach to school development, underpinned by flourishing of expertise and hope, as opposed to deficit and blame. Deterministic notions of 'ability' provide an unacceptable excuse for lack of social mobility and opportunity, yet much current assessment practice unwittingly reinforces this.

Gratifyingly, the ideas and principles of *Learning without Limits* are beginning to gain momentum. Recognition is growing that labelling is unjust. Building a positive state of mind, where colleagues refuse to see children as predictable or their future inevitable, offers a powerful alternative concept. When professional learning flourishes in a culture of trust, teachers are able to put aside limiting notions of 'fixed ability' both for their students and themselves. The development of trust is a key principle of *Learning without Limits*. Without trust, children and teachers feel unable to take risks, to learn effectively and to collaborate. In schools where both children and adults have a sense of agency, an alternative form of school improvement is possible.

This book explores assessment practice that offers an enlightening and enabling view of *all* learners. Children from schools across England have shared their views and offer powerful insights into what may be achieved when limits are lifted on learning. Throughout the book we meet school leaders and teachers who are struggling against practices that seek to define, label and rank. Those who have contributed have taken the opportunity to view assessment reform as a means of reducing inequity through collaboration, professional learning and inquiry. A liberating, alternative view of assessment is presented; achieved through children and adults, working in partnership. Practical examples are offered, illustrated by real-life stories, often about children who have achieved more than their teachers thought possible. (Pseudonyms have been used for children, but the majority of teachers and schools are named.) We begin by considering the dispositions needed by leaders and teachers to support a generous view of educability.

The label of school 'failure'

When I first became headteacher at Wroxham, the school had been defined as 'failing' by inspectors for three years. Hope had been lost, children were disaffected, behaviour was a mixture of passive, bored compliance in classrooms and violence in the playground. The curriculum was massively over-dominated by preparation for tests in English and mathematics and the overriding culture was one of exhaustion and fear. Teachers and children had lost any sense of agency in pursuit of doing what they were told, in anticipation of testing, termly inspection and constant performance review by external advisers. The dilapidated learning environment gave the impression of exhaustion.

In order to make a difference, a sense of optimism fuelled by genuine improvement was needed. I set about working with the school team, the children and wider community in the manner that I had always worked as a teacher. When I reflect now on the concurrent steps that were needed, they look like this:

1   Build an inclusive culture of trust, partnership and listening.
2   Empower teachers' agency through professional learning.
3   Enable pedagogy that finds a way through for every learner (child and adult).
4   Offer an irresistible curriculum.
5   Engage in dialogue that informs future learning and assessment where no one is labelled or limited.

These are the areas that are examined throughout this book, with recognition that each aspect is interconnected. There is little point in focusing on one area without paying attention to the others. However, it is my belief that building a culture of trust is the single most important action that is needed before genuine, sustained learning can flourish. This is particularly challenging in a school that has been labelled as 'failing'. Morale is likely to be low, workload will be relentless and a temptation to blame others may feel inevitable. Joining Wroxham as a new headteacher, not only did I need to trust in the essential *goodness* of colleagues and children, I needed to behave in a manner that meant I would *gain* trust. This process is one that cannot be ignored, as trust that may be hard-won is very easily lost. While engaging in the challenging business of trying to re-inspire the learning community at Wroxham I had precious little time for anything, let alone an opportunity to sit back and reflect on my leadership style. Everything felt instinctive and from the heart.

However, when we began to research the school for *Creating Learning without Limits* it became apparent that seven key dispositions were at play that enabled the school to improve and grow. These dispositions are those that underpin good leadership but apply equally to teaching. Within a school improvement context, they increase capacity for professional learning within an inclusive climate of trust and co-agency. These dispositions are:

- openness to ideas;
- questioning, restlessness and humility;
- inventiveness allowing for creativity;
- persistence and professional courage;
- emotional stability enabling risk-taking;
- generosity that welcomes difference and diversity;
- empathy offering mutual supportiveness.

If we trust that colleagues want to do their best, we are placed in a leadership position that can afford to be open, creative and empathic. It feels enabling to lead from a position of ambitious optimism with faith in others. Very seldom has this approach let me down and these were the very same dispositions that underpinned my classroom practice. Every teacher is a leader of learning.

While gathering research for this book, I have been encouraged by many examples of school leaders internationally who have inspired their schools to achieve excellence through empowering innovation. One such principal is Barb Alaalatoa, who transformed Sylvia Park School in Auckland – predominantly populated by Maori children – from a 'sink school' to one of the greatest success stories in New Zealand. When I asked for the secret of her leadership success, she revealed it was primarily built on relentless energy, optimism, community engagement or *mutukaroa*, and total trust that amazing things happen when we work together, believing that anything is possible.

In Thailand, Ban Khayang Pattana School was established by the Mae Fa Luang Foundation in an opium-growing mountainous region on the borders of Myanmar. The vision of this Royal Foundation was that the hill tribe communities would support education if they were given an opportunity to work for a newly established cooperative. Schools such as these, all over the world, are beginning to recognize the transformability of building communities empowered by trust. As Robin Alexander memorably stated in the final report of the *Cambridge Primary Review*: 'Pupils will not learn to think for themselves if their teachers are expected to do as they are told' (2010: 308).

Leading for *Learning without Limits*

Inspired by the importance of *Learning without Limits* and dispositions that enable professional learning, Paul Browning (2014), an Australian principal, shares his research findings here about leadership and the importance of building trust. He had previously experienced the devastating impact that lack of trust can have within a school. As principal, he wanted to understand and learn more about the behaviours highly trusted leaders exhibit. Through the Queensland University of Technology he engaged in a doctoral research project in 2013 which studied four highly trusted transformational school leaders in depth. He was interested to measure trust, organizational culture and transformational leadership. Browning's research revealed that each of the four school leaders who were the focus of the study were trusted to some degree: some less, and some more than others. His research also revealed that each school had a degree of organizational trust, but there was a clear correlation between the level or degree of trust in the headteacher and the level of organizational trust. The greater the degree of trust in the headteacher, the greater the levels of trust among the teachers.

Intriguingly, the research revealed that trust was not associated with tenure, dispelling the myth that trust is built over time. One of the headteachers studied had only been leading his school for a year. Of the four headteachers, two were female, two were male; two were introverts, two were extroverts. They each led large schools with over 140 staff. Trust is relational; that is to say it is far easier to build trust when you have the opportunity and time to grow individual relationships. However, this study was not interested in 'relational trust' but in leadership behaviour that engendered trust.

We know from other studies that trust has a significant impact on organizational performance and therefore on student achievement. Blasé and Blasé (2001) identified that in a high trust environment teachers felt motivated, satisfied and confident, were more likely to work harder, be optimistic and to feel a sense of professionalism. They found that an environment of trust raised teachers' self-esteem, commitment and sense of ownership. In their longitudinal study of 400 Chicago elementary schools in the 1990s, researchers Anthony Bryk and Barbara Schneider (2002) found that schools with high levels of trust were far more likely to see greater increases in academic outcomes than schools with low levels of trust.

Browning's study (2014) into highly trusted transformational school leaders revealed similar findings to Bryk and Schneider's research (2002) in that a causal analysis of the national test data for the four schools showed outstanding student test performance. These results had been achieved, in no insignificant part, by the creation of a culture of trust rather than a culture of performance measurement and fear. When a school's performance is poor, many leaders default to what they believe will yield quick, turnaround results: they become punitive, seeking to control people through manipulation or coercion. This experience is illustrated later when we hear the story of a brand-new headteacher, impatient for school improvement. Control through fear rarely, if ever, results in lasting positive change. Lasting change and profound positive impact are achieved through the establishment and embedding of trust, a core principle of *Learning without Limits*.

Browning spent a week in each of the four schools, listening to stories told by the staff as to why they trusted their leader. The leaders were shadowed and then the data was triangulated through a whole-staff survey. The study was looking for practices that engendered people's trust, it was not looking for characteristics like integrity or honesty, or particular personality traits, but actions these leaders performed day in and day out that could be emulated by other leaders.

Ten key leadership practices that build trust

After studying all four leaders, a cross-case analysis revealed 10 key practices that effectively built trust and had a positive impact on school culture and, ultimately, student performance. Browning (2014) explains:

> It is important to understand that trust is a socially constructed phenomenon; it means different things for different people. For this reason there can be no commonly agreed definition for trust. For the person who has been through a traumatic marriage break up, discovering that their spouse was having an affair, trust is closely associated with its opposite: betrayal. For the person who has had their personal story shared without their permission by someone they were willing to be vulnerable with, trust is about keeping confidences. For others it is associated with decision-making and the opportunity to have a say in the things that will impact them. No single trust building practice is more important than another. When leading a diverse group of people, each with their own life story and experiences, who have come together in a community to educate young people, all ten leadership practices are equally important.

1 Admit your mistakes

Leaders are not infallible; they are human. How leaders deal with the mistakes they make sets the tone for the rest of the organisation and is a practice in the creation of trust. A leader's willingness to display her vulnerabilities, both personally and professionally, engenders a staff's admiration and trust. Staff members view this practice not as a weakness but as a key strength of leadership, connecting them to their leader on a very human level.

The willingness to be vulnerable, to have the ability to be self-reflective and recognise one's own strengths and weaknesses, to apologise when an error has been made or to reverse a poor decision, portrays the leader's *humility*.

2 Offer trust

No one likes to be micro-managed. Teachers are trained professionals. One of the most powerful actions for gaining the trust of others is to firstly give it. For leaders this means taking a risk and trusting in others first. All four headteachers studied saw a key responsibility of their role as building the empowerment of staff, through the offering of trust. Consequently staff members valued being appreciated and treated like colleagues and professionals, knowing that the headteacher was there in the background if they needed support and advice. The benefits of offering trust went beyond the empowerment of staff to perform their roles; it encouraged many staff members to extend themselves and grow professionally.

3 Actively listen

Highly trusted leaders practise *empathic listening*. This type of listening is about opening yourself to the talker, seeking to identify what they are truly trying to say, to the point where you can actually feel what they are feeling. In the opinion of the staff members at each school studied, the headteacher listened far more than they spoke. They had the ability not to be distracted, to give eye contact, ask clarifying questions, and listen carefully not just to what was said verbally but also for the words that were not uttered. They were then able to demonstrate that they had *heard* by repeating back to the person what was said, identifying succinctly the issue and the emotions felt.

4 Provide affirmation

We all have an innate desire to be appreciated and valued. Bryk and Schneider's research (2002) found that organisations that excel at employee recognition are 12 times more likely to generate strong results than those that do not.

All four headteachers studied employed a range of appreciation strategies including publicly thanking a member of staff at a staff meeting, sending an email or a handwritten thank-you note, leaving a basket of fruit in a staff room to thank people for extra effort, or simply speaking to a person privately to affirm them. Acknowledgement was not only given for significant contributions, but also for the small things a person had done. Teachers found affirmation very motivating, leading to a strengthening of trust because it left them with the impression that their leader knew them and the work they did.

5   Be consultative in decision-making

Highly trusted leaders made informed and consultative decisions. Some decisions have to be made promptly. Staff members often need an answer straight away; invariably a good decision maker is able to do that if the issue warrants it. However, for larger decisions, or decisions that will potentially impact others, trusted leaders use a consultative process, ensuring that the views of all stakeholders are valued and taken into account. Interestingly, trust is not linked to the need to receive an affirmative decision. A leader's ability to be transparent and provide justification for a decision builds trust from the staff, even if the decision is a negative one.

6   Be visible

The administrative load of a headteacher can easily keep them confined to their office. Being visible to the school community is an effective strategy for building trust between a leader and her staff. Many teachers interviewed reported how much they valued seeing the headteacher around the school grounds, speaking with parents, students and individual staff, modelling and reinforcing behaviours and expectations. They also commented on how much they valued the leader's presence in the staff room, at school assemblies, functions and performances. Teachers trusted their leader because she was part of the school; they could see that she was committed to the fundamental purpose of the school and its values. For many teachers visibility is linked to the accessibility of the leader. Staff of trusted leaders not only *see* the headteacher but know that they are accessible to them. Leaders who are inaccessible cannot possibly expect to be trusted, just because they have a title.

7   Keep a consistent demeanour

A consistent, predictable manner and approach to situations, engenders the trust of staff. People by nature want to know what they are going to get. If their leader acts in a reasonable and predictable way people will respect and trust them.

Each of the leaders studied possessed the ability to control their emotions and remain calm and level-headed.

8   Coach and mentor staff

What is important to staff members is the investment on the part of their headteacher in their professional development. As a result, staff members become empowered to manage difficult situations themselves. The practice of coaching and mentoring includes the giving of constructive feedback, which many teachers interviewed during the study said they valued. They saw it as being a vital part of their professional growth.

9   Offer care and concern

Schools by their very nature are relationship-orientated organizations. Philo-sophically, education is about the relationships teachers develop with the students, enabling each student to flourish as a human. The same is true for the relationships between staff; a positive, vibrant school culture is not possible without effective working relationships built on trust. Headteach-ers of the four participating schools extended a genuine care for individual members of their staff. The role of a headteacher is an extremely busy and demanding one, it is hard to find the time to show a genuine concern for an individual, but these highly trusted leaders did.

10   Keep confidences

The final trust engendering practice is confidentiality. In any kind of rela-tionship, confidentiality is essential to maintaining trust. When others have entrusted a person with private or sensitive information they have a moral obligation to honour that trust; the breach of confidentiality may cost that relationship. Trust for individual staff members comes from knowing that they can share personal information with their leader, safe in the knowledge that unless they grant permission, it will not go any further.

What happens when leadership theory doesn't meet reality?

Strikingly, Browning's research findings mirror many of the leadership disposi-tions that we researched at Wroxham for *Creating Learning without Limits*. The important qualities of empathy, emotional stability and humility cannot be over-stated. Creating an inclusive culture of opportunity where children and teachers know they are trusted to learn sounds straightforward and achievable. However, within a climate of stringent accountability measures, there is relentless pressure for speed and quantifiable evidence of improvement. Last year I met Claire at a conference. She was finding her first year of headship incredibly difficult. She had theorized prior to her appointment that she would trust and empower her staff, inspiring them to be creative. However, the pressure of accountability and impending inspection had led her down a different path. With painful honesty, she shares her story here. Her name and the names of her colleagues have been changed.

'I think it went wrong from the first day really . . .'

Claire took up her first headship at the beginning of the spring term. She had read lots of books about leadership and discussed her new role at length with a friend who was a management consultant. She studied all the school information, such as published assessment data and school improvement reports, but only visited the school once, when she was invited to attend the Christmas Nativity. She found the first visit very nerve-wracking, as it was her first view of the parents. Claire recalls that she had a very clear idea of what she wanted the school to be like in the future but thought she should resist making changes for at least a term so she could see what was happening and make informed decisions. She reflected: *'I had a 90-day plan, but it didn't happen the way I had planned at all!'*

Prior to starting her new role, Claire invited all the governors and the senior leadership team to visit the school she was leaving, so they could see what her current school had achieved and what was 'outstanding'. She experienced an enjoyable session with her new governors, creating a three-year vision for an outstanding creative school that would be truly child-focused. Once she took up post, however, Claire began to feel that she had to improve things immediately. The school had an Ofsted judgement of 'requires improvement' and the staff were 'demoralized and disillusioned'. The school had a very poor reputation locally and Claire could see this needed to change. Another inspection was due in the autumn, so although she had theorized about the importance of taking time to build trust and learn about the school, suddenly it felt as though time was not on her side.

'It was such a mess and so scary'

Looking back, Claire commented ruefully, *'I think it all went wrong from the first day really'*. She went into the school during the Christmas holiday before term began, as she wanted to sort the office. She had expected this to take a day or so, but uncovered *'a disorganized and seriously worrying mess'*. She found that documents were in disarray, performance management records were incomplete and confidential paperwork was scattered everywhere. There were files and shelves *'full of stuff that should have been dealt with'*. She began the daunting task of shredding mountains of paperwork from decades ago. Her overriding feeling at that time was that: *'It was such a mess and so scary'*. Claire enlisted the support and help of her family and spent days sorting paper:

> I had known I was taking on a challenge, but trawling through the office cupboards had shown me a fundamental lack of management structures and processes. I did have a working office by the first day of term, but also a sinking feeling about what else I might find. I knew I had to start with safeguarding.

The first day was a training day and Claire was keen to inspire the staff, so they spent time agreeing a new strapline to go with the school logo and discussing what the school was about. However, alongside this, she felt she had to *'lay down the non-negotiables that had to happen to ensure standards'*. To set expectations and in order to illustrate how this was possible, Claire brought books from the outstanding school she had left, for the staff to look at and discuss. Although she intended for this to be an empowering experience, it became a powerful message that there should be 'no excuses'. Despite her intentions, she overlooked the importance of building relationships and trust.

Claire recalls that initially the staff were very nice and were keen to give her the history of why the school was in difficulty. They had had nearly four years without leadership. The last headteacher had been ill and it had taken years before he realized that he needed to move on. Then there had been a temporary headteacher appointed who was only in the school for three days a week and came from a very small school. She had done some good things to stablize the school, but the need for clear leadership was obvious. Listening to the staff, Claire could see why things had become so bad, but resisted the idea that this provided an 'excuse'.

After the training day she went around the school and couldn't help herself from commenting on the 'mess' everywhere:

> I think I was very scared of appearing weak and so I came across as very direct. The school had an air of neglect and disorganization. None of the classrooms provided a reflective and active learning environment. It felt far from the creative child-centred buzz I wanted to create. I quickly found that I had to be crystal clear about what I meant. So instead of implying 'this classroom isn't a great learning environment', I had to say outright, 'You need to get rid of the shelves full of files, clear the window sills, get pencils for every child, put up a clear learning wall . . .'

Establishing relationships was tricky. Every time she said something, however minor, it was reported to everyone and then she would get a reason or excuse back. Claire spent all her time walking around the school, dropping in and out of classrooms. Within the first week she changed lots of procedures and systems. If she asked why things were happening as they did, she would be told, 'Because it's always been like that!'

Without trust

It was a very lonely first term. In order to build what was so clear in her mind, Claire decided that she had to start with being 'very direct'. However, it became obvious to Claire that the staff genuinely didn't know how to achieve what she was talking about. Some were desperate to improve and others were not so keen:

> I think that my role became very managerial and not at all inspirational, as I felt forced to focus on procedures and 'musts'. Every time I carried out lesson observations, giving feedback was a challenge. I became someone I never wanted to be as I held people to account, but could rarely praise.

Claire tried to listen to the staff and in response provided many training sessions that focused on 'what good learning looks like and how to do it'. She found herself dictating what should be in each classroom and she constantly talked about learning. At the same time, she talked to staff about accountability and began addressing teachers who were not performing. Deadlines were set and Claire insisted they were met. Every time she found an issue, she discussed this publicly so everyone knew what was *'incorrect and what was fine'*. She addressed all the reasons given by her teachers for 'poor lessons' and learning. Teachers' lack of subject knowledge became evident as they tried to introduce the new curriculum and she increased the amount of training still further, so that she could be sure teachers had been given every chance to succeed.

> *I tried so hard to get staff to buy into the vision by sharing my plans and by reassuring them that I wasn't going anywhere and that I would fight anyone for them if they were doing a good job. They were worn down by visits from local authority officers, support partners, HMI, telling them about different methodology and ideas; usually focusing on action, but not embedding understanding of 'how' or 'why'. I sent teachers to visit other schools and covered classes myself to show them I could and would. I watched teaching assistants and then organized training straight away (which I paid them to attend), so I could try to put right what I observed.*

Claire rapidly became 'bogged down' in very difficult personnel issues both in performance management and in trying to restructure staffing that she felt had previously been organized for the convenience of adults instead of children. She remembers days when she 'really just wanted to walk away' but then reminded herself that 'the children were great' and increasingly she believed that the school had potential.

Engaging the children

Claire introduced Guy Claxton's work on *Building Learning Power* (2002) and ensured that through assemblies and celebrations she emphasized to the children that the school was now focused on learning and that their learning behaviour was now valued. Positive energy from the children began to encourage her:

> *I went into classrooms where pupils rushed up to me tell me how they had been resilient in solving a problem, or how they were managing distractions. With relief, I began to see that this approach was starting to make a difference.*

She started to tackle the culture of low expectations of behaviour. This remains a huge focus but has begun to improve already and Claire is keen to give more responsibility to the children. She has trained peer mediators (see the description of peer mediation in Chapter 2, pp. 21–3) and aims to introduce child 'learning detectives' in the near future.

> *The hardest thing was not having anyone to offload onto. As time went on I thought I had uncovered everything, then I would find that another layer would materialize and I had to make decisions alone. I found the office a good place to hide when it was too much. Keeping my temper in check and masking emotion was extremely hard.*

'Gradually momentum began to build'

Claire modelled what she wanted in classrooms and throughout the school and, with constant communication about the vision, some staff began to come to her to ask advice. This was a real turning point and she spent a lot of time with a few teachers planning lessons and discussing concepts. She helped set up classrooms and cleaned out cupboards, and gradually momentum began to build.

At the same time, she began capability support plans and had frank discussions with other teachers. She could see the school changing and so could parents and governors. A local authority monitoring visit was a real high as the officer actually got so excited about the changes that were visible that she gave Claire a hug: *'Her report was something I needed desperately as she had been coming to the school for many years and was so aware of the problems. Her opinion really counted.'*

Claire made links with another local headteacher who had taken a school from an Ofsted judgement of 'requires improvement' to 'good':

> *She has become the person I need who I can trust and will help me when I don't know what to do. I email her at ridiculous hours and she always answers, so I know I'm not the only person who doesn't have any life apart from school. My governors have been incredible. They really know the school and have been very supportive so far! I have really needed their support, especially with the personnel issues that have arisen. There are times now when I feel excited. The staff who remain want to be with me. They are beginning to talk about learning and have really raised their game. The school looks different. It is no longer messy and disorganized – we have just filled the seventh skip!*

The turning point

There are no short cuts to building trust and empowerment. There was one teacher, Wendy, who Claire initially had a difficult time with. Wendy was put on a support plan, went off sick, but then returned. The targets on the support plan were met and suddenly Claire felt that a mutual understanding had been achieved. Wendy has since told her that she was very direct and abrupt when she first began to observe and Claire realizes she was right:

> *I was so overwhelmed, that I think I defaulted to serious and stern. If I had my time over, I would try hard not to repeat this and have learnt to fix a smile to my face even when my stomach is quivering. I am grateful that this teacher has changed, taken on board advice about her teaching and has decided to stay as I feel less bad about those colleagues who decided our school was not the place for them. I know there are still massive problems but I can now walk around my school and see many more good lessons and I can see children who are proud of their achievements and can talk excitedly about learning. I can see books with great evidence of progress. The creativity is beginning and energy is building. I have to be patient and not worry about Ofsted who will visit next term, but focus on the outstanding school we can create together. I have learnt so much and made some big mistakes in handling people, but I feel that the pieces of this very complex jigsaw are starting to fit together. I hope I am right.*

At the time of writing, Claire has appointed three new teachers to start at the school and is optimistic that they share her vision. After two terms of struggle, Claire is beginning to see the benefit of building relationships and trust in order that the school can start to flourish.

What has leadership got to do with assessment?

I am grateful to Claire for sharing this account. It is tempting from the outside to read about her actions and see how she might have acted differently, informed by Browning's leadership practices that build trust. However, her account illustrates the challenge of leadership and the risks of isolation and conflict when time feels too compressed to work collaboratively. The experience that Claire had with her staff is one that teachers may experience with their class. Too often, external pressure forces an imperative for speed of improvement at all costs. In many schools, teachers are expected to achieve apparent improvement by showing measurable progress. Tracking scores that appear to show a rapid upward trajectory do not necessarily provide evidence of genuine sustained learning.

This book explores an alternative perspective of assessment and learning that is predicated on the view that when teachers work in partnership with children in a spirit of ambition, organizing high-quality learning experiences, amazing things happen. Leaders are crucial in creating opportunities for everyone within school to flourish. Risks need to be taken, trust needs to be real. Transformability is possible when the atmosphere within a school has a palpable feel of excitement fuelled by intellectual rigour, creativity and ambition for every child. These are the ingredients of an excellent learning environment for both children and teachers. It is possible to create this climate within individual classrooms but when leaders are able to build this across a whole learning community, the impact is truly life changing.

Summary

As we have seen, creating a leadership culture of trust and opportunity is complex and takes time. It is easy to recognize the positive impact of reciprocal trust, but far more difficult to achieve. However, building and sustaining trust is of vital importance within an overall ambition of creating a school where limits can be lifted on the learning of both children and adults. There is an important parallel between the role of headteacher establishing trust among her staff team and the teacher building a learning relationship with her class. In both cases, much more can be achieved if a spirit of partnership and collective ambition is built.

In Chapter 2, we consider the importance of listening to children as a means of finding a way to support every learner towards success, as opposed to a narrow instrumental view of school as a machine for the production of test scores.

2

Learning to listen: Finding a way through for every child

Don't be scared of what you can do – you can show the whole world if you want to.

(Helen, 10 years old)

In *Creating Learning without Limits* (Swann et al. 2012) we reflected on the liberating idea of learning capacity as opposed to fixed 'ability'. If we free ourselves to imagine an ambitious future for learners, we are most likely to achieve this through working in partnership. Co-agency between teachers and learners is at the heart of a pedagogy that resists limits. Building a culture of trust in order that teachers are valued and empowered is also imperative, as discussed in Chapter 1. When teachers are trusted, they are more likely to be open to listening and responding to children. Schools that enable listening and meaningful dialogue about learning establish whole-school structures that support that ethos. In this chapter we consider initiatives within schools to encourage pupil voice and also learn of the transformative impact upon individual children where a culture of co-agency has been established. In later chapters we discuss classroom organization without 'ability' grouping and the opportunities this provides for formative assessment dialogue that builds intrinsic motivation. This emancipatory approach to the leadership of learning enables surprising levels of achievement.

Connections in learning are crucially important to developing cognition. Often, through dialogue, we gain insight into the child's emerging understanding in a way that cannot possibly be substituted through passive post-learning activity such as scrutinizing children's exercise books. It is important, therefore, to give children the opportunity to express their emerging understanding in a safe and non-judgemental environment. This environment should be founded on trust and include every member of the class. Dialogue is a medium through which children can make better sense of 'big ideas' through sharing their developing understanding, revising their ideas and exploring differences in perspective. However, playing with new ideas in order to achieve greater insight is unlikely to take place unless the classroom offers a safe place to do this.

We place great emphasis, at Wroxham, on the importance of listening to children. We recognize the impact that dialogue between children and adults can have for everybody within a class, once predetermined outcomes have been put aside. Our pedagogical approach is to model language that provides subject-specific vocabulary and technical terms in order that children can begin to use these words and phrases in their own talk. The importance of the spoken word, development of dialogue and debate are central to teaching throughout the school. Daily opportunities are provided for children to engage in conversation about their learning and to develop their thinking through discussing ideas. Recently, some Year Four children participated in lessons aimed at specifically teaching dialogic skills. Phillipson and Wegerif (forthcoming) use the following structure to enable children to see the combined processes involved in meaningful dialogue. They describe the essential harmony between these four modes of thinking:

1   **Caring** – involving and valuing the contribution of others and showing concern for their joint endeavour.
2   **Collaborative** – supporting each other to build shared understanding.
3   **Critical** – questioning ideas, demanding reasons and evidence, making judgements.
4   **Creative** – putting forward hypotheses, finding examples and alternatives and synthesizing ideas.

Creating an environment in which children can safely share, question and explore their emerging understanding provides a rich context for assessment. The children's ideas, interests and misconceptions, and the language they use to explore them, become 'visible' to themselves, their peers and the teacher.

The importance of dialogue

Robin Alexander's (2008) extensive work on the role of dialogue to extend both thought and understanding recognizes that dialogue should be collective, reciprocal, supportive, cumulative and purposeful. He identifies dialogic teaching principles that underpin dialogue that values both the teacher *and learner*. Any teacher that seeks to engage children in conversation about learning and formative assessment therefore needs to value the spoken word as the prime means of communication. From children's earliest days in the Foundation Stage at Wroxham, we seek to provide meaningful opportunities for them to take decisions and talk about their ideas. This ethos builds throughout the school and includes whole-school strategies such as 'circle meeting groups' designed to ensure all voices are heard.

Organizational structures that facilitate listening

We move on now to explore the kinds of whole-school structures and initiatives that can be put in place to facilitate democratic engagement and to ensure that listening results in action. Establishing a culture of trust where it is safe to explore ideas means enabling many voices within the school community to be heard.

Every Tuesday morning throughout term time, mixed-age circle meetings take place at The Wroxham School. The meetings are planned and led by Year Six children with adults in attendance as part of the circle. The meeting lasts for 15 minutes before mid-morning playtime. Helen and Polly from Year Six explain how the groups work:

> **Polly:** *I think with circle groups, like with play-leading, it is quite nice to lead and to have your turn, because everyone in the school has a turn of leading circle groups when they are in Year Six and it is nice to see everyone's views. Last time we said, 'Think of all the words you use in maths' and we can see what all the younger children have learned and can come up with and it's good to see what they've learned in their year. We go round in a circle and ask each person and if they can't come up with an idea, we come back to them so everyone gets a turn.*
>
> **Helen:** *We are split into seven groups across the school, with all the classes mixed up. We start with a warm-up and we get the children a little bit active before we start, basically a simple warm-up and we get into the news of what's going to happen later in the day or next week or something and then the topic of discussion is like, 'What can we do to improve the school?'*

Other Year Six circle group leaders explain:

> **Evie:** *I think that it's good because you can work with all years. Everyone gets a go at speaking. Sometimes we go round in a circle, sometimes we put our hands up, it's just different – yes.*
>
> **John:** *Like in peer mediation, you have to listen to what other people say and write down what they say even if it is out of the ordinary, you still write it down because it might be useful in the next circle group.*
>
> **Nida:** *It's also good, so you can get really good friends in other classes because all the classes come together and you get to know people more through talking and playing games and then you also get to know what's major in the school and there's topic of discussion that helps the headteacher and teachers figure out what's important.*
>
> **Karen:** *If younger ones are not saying too much, we would ask them what they think and what they think is important.*

Nida: *We say things like, 'Is there anyone who would like to contribute?' Or 'Does anyone have anything to add to this conversation?' If we see someone who wants to say something, but they are not very brave, we can just go round in a circle to get all the ideas first.*

Karen: *Sometimes they say 'pass' and we come back to them when they have had more time to think.*

Nida: *In Year Six you have more responsibility because you have to lead them but in the other years you just have to listen and contribute ideas.*

Jerry: *I remember looking up to our Year Six when I was in Year Five, Year Four, Year Three and below, we would see how they would run it and it definitely helped us. You start it when you are in Year One so you have a few years to see how different Year Six leaders do it, so by the time you get there you have your own ideas about how you want to run it.*

This kind of whole-school structure raises an expectation that ideas will be shared and that there is a continual opportunity to make school a dynamic place where everyone is valued. One such idea was presented to the whole school in an assembly planned and delivered by two Year Four girls, Maisie and Caitlin. Inspired by the work their parents were doing as part of an environmental group within the school, they searched the internet for examples of playgrounds with interesting, environmentally-friendly play spaces. They produced a mood board and wrote a presentation that included ideas such as a recycling station for food waste and rubbish, a picnic area, a performance area, an underground tunnel, a weather station and a slide. The children went on to discuss these ideas in circle groups, funds from the Christmas Fair were allocated by the Wroxham Friends Association and work has now begun in the playground. A listening culture enables energy to build around emerging ideas in anticipation that change will take place. The whole-school nature of mixed-age circle groups leads to greater impact, demonstrating the power of citizenship as a lived experience (Peacock 2011, 2012).

Peer mediation

An extension of the ethos of mixed-age circle meetings at Wroxham is the provision of trained Year Six peer mediators who are available on the playground each day to try to resolve differences between those in younger classes. Volunteers from Year Six sign up to a weekly rota and wear bright-red bibs. All children in Year Six receive a half-day of training from their teachers about building skills of mediation and conflict resolution. During training the children engage in drama and structured role-play activities to rehearse the structure of peer mediation. Following the training morning, an assembly is arranged for all children from Years One to Year Five so that the newly-trained mediators can explain their role to the rest of the school.

The mediators (usually two children) have a quiet space to meet with the children who have a disagreement. They explain to the younger children that the purpose of the meeting is to reach agreement. The children are first reminded of the process:

- each person will explain what happened;
- no one will interrupt while explanations are being given;
- the privacy of the conversation should be respected.

The mediators then tell the children that they promise:

- we will not take sides;
- we will not tell anyone what to do;
- we will only talk to an adult if we are concerned or cannot resolve the problem.

The conversation between mediators and younger children is structured so that the mediators ask each child in turn to explain what has happened and then repeat this in summary to check for understanding and to clarify the feelings and position of each child. Year Six mediators explain:

> *We promise not to share the argument with other people but if we are really worried we will tell the teachers . . . if the problem is really big the teachers sort it out. Sharing is usually the problem, such as 'Who had this ball first?'*

> (Lisa, Year Six)

John reflects:

> *You have to listen to both sides, you have to respect what other people say . . . you help them but you don't get too much involved; if it's really serious get a teacher, if it's not too serious you should be able to sort it out and write it in the folder.*

Hayley comments that peer mediation is necessary *'Because there might be arguments on the playground that the teachers don't know about because it might be a hidden argument.'* The notion of 'hidden arguments' that may only be discovered by other children is interesting and illustrates the value of trusting children to support each other. Emotional development and empathy are also enhanced through the peer mediation process:

> *I feel quite happy when I have sorted out an argument because you have just fixed someone's problem instead of someone just keeping it in their*

mind because it's hard to go to sleep if you have something on your mind that is bothering you.

(Karen, Year Six)

At the end of lunchtime, any incidents are noted and filed.

Emotional well-being and safety is another key feature of schools where co-agency flourishes. When children know they are trusted and are safe, they are ready to take risks with trying out new things. This is essential for learning and is a key part of a school culture where self-assessment is encouraged. In addition to peer mediation, a lunchtime nurture group runs each day welcoming children who may find the playground overwhelming. There is also a daily art club, sports coaching and the opportunity to read on the playground double-decker bus. Recognition that children need different spaces for leisure and play is respectful of individual needs and enables everyone to feel valued. Art therapy is also offered for children and occasionally for staff. The importance of providing a containing environment cannot be overestimated.

All the schools that have contributed stories of their assessment practice to this book also value their approach to listening to children, and in the next section of this chapter we consider some examples. For instance, in recognition of the importance of pupil voice, many schools have organized school councils or other forms of consultative groups that seek to gain insight from the opinions and comments of children.

Listening to children

Bridgewater School learning conferences

Bridgewater School in Northampton summarizes learning achievement in partnership with children through termly learning conferences. Alison Harvey, headteacher, writes:

> *Nurture is vital at Bridgewater, as if a child's emotional intelligence is not in the right place then they aren't going to achieve in their learning that day, or for a while and won't be in a place to take risks or challenges. The children understand what support there is for them and appreciate the daily nurture lunch where you can go with a friend, where there is always an adult to support if required. This enables them to have the confidence to manage their well-being and therefore retain the ability to meet challenges in their learning and keep them on track.*

Park Street School whole-school forum

When headteacher Tina Facer joined Park Street School in Hertfordshire, she began by establishing the vision for the school. Staff and governors discussed the attributes they wanted children to have developed by the end of Year Six. These were then framed as values, aims and a motto. Having done this, the staff collected ideas about how the aims could be achieved. It was suggested that establishing a whole-school forum would be a way forward as this would enable every voice to be heard and valued. The meetings are held once a month and all members of the school community attend. Year Six children run the meetings and write the minutes. They have become practised at ensuring that even the quiet or shy children feel comfortable enough to share their opinions. Out of these meetings have come many other initiatives: mixed playtimes (younger and older children mixing on playgrounds), a sports festival rather than a traditional sports day, more of a mix of approaches to teaching and learning, innovative ideas to celebrate book week and a 'Japanese Day'. After a year of trialling this approach the children were asked to evaluate its effectiveness:

> *Having a whole-school forum is a good idea as you get to hear everyone's opinion from around the school.*

> *I like [the] forum because everyone joins in.*

> *It works well because it lets everyone have a say in what happens to our school.*

> *It gives everyone a voice.*

> *There are more ideas and more voices to be heard.*

> *Everybody gets a say and everybody is part of our school.*

> *It is a good thing because we can decide as a whole school not just the teachers deciding what we do all the time.*

Moss Hey School learning council

Moss Hey School in Stockport also takes pupil voice seriously and recently established a learning council to enable pupils to actively participate in improving the school community. Tabitha Smith, headteacher, says the learning council gives children the opportunity to express their thoughts and opinions about learning and school life, in a forum where they feel comfortable, are listened to and know action will be taken. Moving beyond a traditional school council, this model incorporates a structure that ensures an open channel of communication between children, the senior management team and the governing body.

> *We take the views of pupils into account when planning changes and developments to the curriculum and learning. Involving children in evaluating*

the curriculum and having an insight into the ways that pupils think about learning can be extremely beneficial. It helps to create a positive learning culture based on trust, improve aspects of pupils' learning and help create new ideas and strategies for teaching.

(Tabitha Smith, headteacher)

The learning council has a prominent display board within the school and produces a termly newsletter so all members of the school community can be kept up to date with council matters. The learning council comprises two children from Years One to Year Six who are democratically elected at the start of the year. They meet on a regular basis during curriculum time and follow an agreed agenda. All council members have a code of conduct to which they agree to abide by and are familiar with the learning council constitution. They are representatives of the school and agree to maintain a high standard of behaviour and to provide positive role models. During meetings, all members understand the importance of listening to the thoughts and opinions of others and everyone feels valued – thus promoting a culture of trust and respect. Learning councillors are given the opportunity to report back from meetings and discuss issues in their classes as part of a class council. By using debates in the classroom, pupils are learning to develop their own opinions and to appreciate the importance of listening to the views of their peers: *'At learning council meetings everyone is listened to and we all have a turn to say what we think'* (Year Six councillor). Councillors have been involved in learning walks around the school, identifying aspects of classrooms that help support their learning and also making valuable suggestions for areas that could be improved. They also carried out a curriculum review, identifying areas they particularly enjoyed and putting forward ideas for new topics to be studied. Topic books have also been evaluated and councillors are able to talk animatedly about their own work and, by listening to others, gain an understanding of learning across the whole school: *'Being a learning councillor is an important job because it means I can tell the teachers what helps me to learn and what I enjoy'* (Year Four councillor). The learning council has also provided teachers and governors with information about issues such as how to provide effective marking and feedback.

In schools like Moss Hey and Park Street we see the development of a culture where children are able to contribute to pedagogical thinking because co-agency is real. It takes time and a climate of trust before children feel confident about commenting on pedagogy.

A 'rights respecting' ethos

Learning about rights, learning through rights and learning for rights within an overall context of education as a right.

(UNICEF UK)

The importance of purposeful dialogue has been further supported and developed at Sunnyfields, Barnet, because it has become a 'rights respecting school'. This national initiative by UNICEF UK supports schools to embed the human rights agreed by the United Nations Convention on the Rights of the Child 1989, ratified by the United Kingdom in 1991. Ann Richards, assistant headteacher, believes that through learning about their rights, the children have also learned about the importance of respecting the rights of others. She believes this has enabled a positive, safe environment for learning to develop. Children at Sunnyfields are willing to meet challenges and are able to view mistakes as a learning opportunity. In his end of year report, 10-year-old Aref proudly mentioned his role as a rights respecting ambassador: *'My class raised a lot of money to help stop child labour. I am proud to be an ambassador and hope to do more.'* This whole-school ethic of listening has transformed the school: *'Our approach has developed responsible articulate pupils who are in charge of their own learning, where barriers to success are replaced by high aspirations and outcomes'* (Ann Richards, assistant headteacher).

Listening to those who find learning difficult

Building a listening culture throughout a school is an essential precursor to engaging learners in dialogue. For children who find school a difficult place to thrive, it is important to explore ways of building an ethos of 'finding a way through' for every child, recognizing that this takes commitment and courage. It can be tempting to look for the deficit and to find reasons why a child finds learning difficult. This kind of thinking can prevent us from believing in the 'art of the possible' and should be avoided at all costs. What is needed is a collective ambition from all those involved with the child to seek a way to unlock her inner capacity to learn. In the following pages we meet children who have been helped to move beyond labels, to achieve more than they or their teachers expected. We begin by hearing from Vanessa Pearce, from Beaudesert Lower School, who describes the insights she gained from working with 8-year-old Henry:

> *Henry is one of the children in my class that I feel epitomizes the benefits of a 'Learning without Limits' ethos and the embodiment of growth mindset. He entered my class a quiet, under-confident child on the pupil premium register, with poor attendance. Reports from his previous teacher and data presented on the school tracking system suggested that Henry had made little or no progress across the board, especially in maths. His previous teacher felt his 'capability was low'. He was said to be two years behind in his learning.*

Vanessa soon realized that Henry's first thought during independent work time was to attempt to copy what his neighbour was doing. He appeared disengaged and seemed to have no belief in his capacity to learn mathematics. At the start of his first week, his progress, motivation and self-belief appeared remarkably low. Tasks were rarely completed and he constantly complained of 'not being very good at maths'. Vanessa recalls that when working with Henry individually or in a small group, it was as though he had had no previous experience of maths lessons. Here was a child who presented 'as a helpless victim in the learning environment'. He did not appear to understand the freedom and autonomy that Vanessa sought to provide for the children in her class. Henry's self-identity as a learner was one of passive failure.

Vanessa ensured she found time to talk individually with Henry in an attempt to engage him in learning, focusing initially on his mathematical development and participation. She showed him how practical approaches with a range of resources could open his understanding and encouraged Henry to share his new practical strategies with other children. Eventually, Henry began to enjoy sharing his learning with the rest of the class:

> *The extent to which Henry began to take on an alternative view of himself as learner and a problem-solver had an impact that was tangible. He began to take control over his learning in maths lessons, because he finally believed that he could. I continued to ensure that Henry was provided with regular opportunities to stretch his emerging sense of empowerment.*

In November, in her role as maths leader, Vanessa organized a whole-school maths meeting for parents. She asked teachers to recommend children from every year group who could demonstrate an aspect of mathematics they had learned about that term. This was her second year as maths leader. The first time she organized the event, she noticed that staff would only send children that they felt were their 'confident mathematicians' – or worse, those 'from my top group'. Dismayed by this, Vanessa made it clearer in her second year that she particularly wanted to celebrate anyone who had overcome a lack of understanding in any aspect of mathematics. Henry was chosen as one of the Year Three learning demonstrators. Vanessa was heartened to see how he 'visibly bloomed' while sharing with the parents how he used a number line to 'find the difference' and demonstrated that he was able to check his answer accurately within a problem-solving context.

Back in class, Henry was very keen to share his maths learning and was thrilled when Vanessa asked him to help another child who needed support. Whenever possible, Vanessa found opportunities to increase Henry's understanding and confidence. This included some individual pre-learning sessions for 30 minutes each Friday afternoon, while other children were engaged in independent activities, which enabled Henry to approach the new week with confidence.

Henry's new sense of 'can-do' as a learner had many positive effects. His writing stamina, imagination and motivation all increased significantly. His attendance became exemplary, to the extent that he would attempt to come to school even if he was ill. He took a new pride in all learning that he was involved in. As Vanessa said,

There were so many proud moments that I felt with Henry. Most gratifying for me, however, was the sentence that he wrote on his feedback sheet for the year. Asked what he had enjoyed in Year Three, Henry wrote:

I have enjoyed everything, especially maths because I'm really good at maths now . . .

This story of Henry's discovery that mathematics was something he could be 'good at' is essentially a story of what happens when, as a learner, your teacher refuses to give up on you. This requires a *Learning without Limits* mindset from the teacher and illustrates the power for transformability that we hold within schools.

Earning Mary's trust

There have been many children at Wroxham that have shown us what is possible in a school where we try never to limit learning. One such story is that of Mary, who continues to surprise us each day with her insight and unique view of the world.

Mary joined our Upper Foundation class at The Wroxham School having not previously attended our nursery. Her mother came to see me to look around the school and to tell me about Mary, who she felt should not join her siblings at their primary school as she did not believe it was a place where Mary would thrive. She explained to me that Mary's special educational needs meant that she needed a school that would understand her individuality and would allow her to achieve on her own terms. We walked around the school together and when we returned to my office, Mary's mother confirmed that she would like to apply for a place for her daughter because: *'I believe you will love her for who she is.'*

When Mary arrived in school, we provided additional classroom support as we had been advised she was liable to have extreme tantrums and could be violent. The reality was that she settled in quickly and enjoyed a wide range of learning through play, both indoors and outdoors. However, she refused to engage in any mark-making activities whatsoever. She would not paint, draw, swirl shaving foam, make patterns in sand – nothing to show us that she could create images; until one day in February when she picked up a whiteboard and black felt pen to draw the image shown in Figure 2.1.

I recall the first time I saw this image; my immediate feeling was one of surprise and delight. Not only had Mary settled well into school, she was happy and now trusted us enough to share her drawings.

I believe Mary's story has a great deal to tell us about early learning and the pitfalls that educationalists can experience if we believe that we can reliably make judgements about learning on the basis of performance within classrooms.

Figure 2.1 Mary's drawing

Clearly this picture is not the first that Mary has ever drawn. It is, however, the first time that she chose to trust those surrounding her in the Upper Foundation classroom to see her drawing. There is an important distinction to be made between 'performance' for an adult agenda that seeks to measure attainment, and genuine learning and insight that is only revealed when the child feels safe enough to open up. In this case, Mary's drawing showed she was ready to trust her teachers.

Transition to secondary school

Another child at Wroxham, Polly, has recently started secondary school. She is thriving in her new environment but could so easily have developed a deficit view of herself as a learner. Her story is one that illustrates the impact of a culture that resists labelling children according to their prowess in reading and writing. She had been in school since nursery, but when we interviewed her at the end of Year Six, she recalled that when she was younger she felt worried about her learning:

> I think most people felt they were very shy and not confident about their work – from the start of Wroxham now coming up to Year Six, I feel like I have improved massively and that I have conquered a lot of fears and I am happy a lot.

This provides a fascinating insight. Polly, a highly motivated learner, richly supported at home, initially found learning to read and write really difficult. Indeed, when she was assessed at the end of Year Two she did not achieve the nationally expected standard of Level 2. What is illuminating, however, is her comment above that assumes *most* people felt they were shy and not confident. She goes on to explain:

> *I think everyone can say they didn't feel like they could fit in a lot and they may feel like I did a lot, that maybe they couldn't do some of the work? But then as they've come up to say Year One and you still think 'I still probably can't do this' and then you start to think 'Oh yes I can do this' and then each year you think 'Oh I've just learned something new there!' and more and then more and then in Year Six you feel like you know it all! But then . . . (although obviously there is more you haven't learnt), that's why it's so good at Wroxham because they make you feel welcome and that when you leave primary school, you leave it with confidence and you are ready to learn new things and think new things.*

Polly has a positive experience of school. She has not been demoralized through being ability-grouped or labelled. She has not been defined by her capacity to perform in tests. She looks back over her experience of school and chuckles, as she reflects that probably 'everybody else' felt that there were things they were struggling to understand. She did not experience feelings of failure or humiliation. This is because she was included within classrooms that eschewed notions of hierarchy based on attainment. She did not give up, nor did others give up on her. When we read her writing in Chapter 5 we see the results of a culture of opportunity, as opposed to ability labelling. In her final learning review meeting (see Chapter 6) she recognized that there were still many areas of English that she needed to 'challenge herself' on but she also celebrated her successes:

> *In English I am very happy with writing a long story – I tried to make it very descriptive and challenge myself and I loved reading my picture story book to Reception. I sometimes struggle with making the tense right in a story and try to keep it the right tense all the way through. Sometimes it's hard making sense in a story, um, like to make it sound right and to make the sentences short and snappy.*

By the time Polly left primary school she had become an avid, fluent reader and a proficient writer. Here, in conversation with her friend Helen, she appears to be gearing herself up, reminding herself that she will be able to overcome challenges that may lie ahead at her new school:

> **Polly:** *There's so many things in Wroxham where you don't feel left out, you can just do it with your friends and with confidence and passion.*

Helen: *Don't be scared of what you can do. You can show the whole world if you want to [laughs] you can show all your teachers what you can do. Go for it! There is nothing to be scared of.*

Polly: *Yes . . . there is nothing that can stop you. Yes and if you feel like you've hit a brick wall and you can't do this, then ask for help from teachers, but also just think back from all the years that you have done and think when you first started you weren't there at all, but when you were in Year One you learnt loads of things and you felt confident. So just keep working hard and you will soon find that you feel you know everything you need, but don't stop working as hard as you can, because it's really good to work hard and show your effort into every piece of work you do.*

Leva finds her voice

At Meredith Infant School in Portsmouth, the school team decided to use film to enhance feedback from children to their families about their learning achievements (see Chapter 6). Sharon Peckham found the use of film enabled much greater understanding about one child's learning in her class. Leva joined the Reception class speaking her home language fluently. She had two English words, 'thank you' (which she pronounced *shthank*) and had a wonderful smile. She was inquisitive about learning and her confidence grew quickly. By the end of the first term she was communicating in English with her friends. By the spring she had developed into 'a wonderful little chatter box'. Leva's dad evidently loved her dearly but his English was limited to a few phrases. He would often arrive at the classroom door to speak to Sharon about Leva and they would both 'bumble through' a conversation, not always quite understanding one another. On parents' evening, dad's main question was, 'Is Leva happy?' He believed her English to be poor, so he worried that she hadn't made friends. He asked about Leva's English, indicating with his hands that it was perhaps, 'okay' at best. Sharon enthusiastically explained that her English was 'fantastic', showing double thumbs up back to dad. As much as she tried to convince dad, Sharon could see he was still worried. So then she pressed play on Leva's video (where we can imagine a happy and bright-eyed little girl confidently chatting away in English). There dad sat, eyes filled with tears, face filled with love and pride, as he watched his daughter chat away. Sharon fought back her emotion but it was hard because she realized that this video had given Leva's dad so much understanding about his daughter and her achievements. It transpired that Leva never spoke English at home, preferring to communicate with her parents in her home language. This was the first time that Leva's father had listened to her English. Dad was later able to share the video with Leva's grandparents abroad who had not seen their granddaughter for two years.

Impact on pedagogy

There is no substitute for children talking about their own learning. For too long, we have accepted a norm that assumes adults should talk and children should listen. In the following brief transcript of dialogue we gain a glimpse of the insight that children can offer into the effectiveness (or otherwise) of teaching. While researching for his higher degree, Luke Rolls, now teaching at the University of Cambridge Primary School, interviewed some 9-year-old children in a London school about their experience of maths lessons:

> **Luke:** *How does that feel when you say the lessons are rushing?*
> **Gina:** *I don't like that. I actually come to school to learn. I don't like it when we do one lesson on adding fractions and then one lesson on something completely different. I actually want to learn it a few times to get it in my head, not just once.*

Permjit expresses his frustration about the apparent lack of time in many classrooms for ideas to be expressed and debated:

> *The thing is with teachers, they try to say everything and so you don't have time. I'm not pointing to you Mr Rolls . . . but the teachers, they could say less, for the children to say more. They do know a lot, but they should say less, because let's say it was them ten years before, they wouldn't want their teacher to say everything because they would want to be learning. You're not really learning that much because the teacher's just giving you everything . . . Arguing is good because you are taking on people's ideas and then it helps you understand. Basically, you should say what you think, see what people say and then think about it.*

This is the kind of feedback that we need to hear from the children we teach and is at the heart of lessons designed to promote philosophical debate. These children are engaging with their teacher as learners in pursuit of optimum opportunities to learn. Once a culture has been established where this depth of dialogue can take place, assessment in the classroom truly has the chance to be the province not only of the teacher but of every child too. In a classroom with 30 children and one teacher there can be 31 assessors. In the next chapter we visit classrooms that exhibit shared responsibility for thinking about learning and assessing understanding.

Summary

In this chapter we have considered structures within schools that support the development of democratic engagement and have seen that children readily engage in deep and meaningful dialogue once they have genuine reasons to do so. Moreover, if we wish children to help us to understand how best to teach them, we need to establish mutual respect through co-agency. Stories of individual children illustrate that empathic listening and openness enables us a greater chance of 'finding a way through' for every child. A culture of listening enables mutual understanding to develop and enables children to make connections, thereby making new leaps in learning. In Chapter 3 we discover ways that the curriculum can enable opportunities for learners and teachers to engage in assessment that enhances understanding.

3

A language for thinking: Assessment through dialogue

If you want every pupil to succeed in their dreams; every heart is needed.

(Alice, Chloe, Rachel and Felicity, 11 years old)

At a recent conference, a panel of 11-year-old children from Year Seven opened the event by sharing insights about their experiences of primary school. Each child spoke with warmth and loyalty about their school but it rapidly emerged that in every case they had experienced a narrowing of the curriculum during their final two years of school, in favour of English and maths lessons in preparation for SATs. One boy revealed that science had not been taught since Year Four and none of the children could recall music or drama lessons in their final year until after the tests in May. The experience of these children echoes the research findings of the *Children, their World, their Education: final report of the Cambridge Primary Review* (Alexander 2010). A lack of coherence and balance in the curriculum leads to an impoverished educational offer. Although what is memorable does not necessarily equate with what is of most value over time, it is interesting to ask children about their overall experience of school. After all, if we seek to inspire lifelong learners we need to do more than attend to the demands of tests and examinations.

Tina Facer, from Park Street School in Hertfordshire, and Kath Burns, from St Nicolas Junior School in West Berkshire, asked their children to comment on their most memorable experiences of primary school before they left for secondary school at the end of the year:

I enjoyed taking 'Poppy Bear' home in Reception.
We went to Southend and I dropped my ice cream in the sea and my teacher bought me another one.
In nursery when I didn't have any friends the teacher showed me James and we are still friends now.

I remember when we had a 1930s day and the teacher acted really strictly when I broke my chalk.

When we were at the top of the giant swing at camp, we were singing 'Let it Go'. As we pulled the rope the word 'go' got louder and louder because we were screaming so much.

I remember when I came back to school with a cast on my arm and Tilly came out of the classroom and saw me. She was so excited that she went back in and told everyone and suddenly there was a crowd of people at the door waving at me.

I remember when we made Viking long boats.

Making pancakes and playing with fire.

Forensic science week – especially blood splattering and fingerprinting.

Our 'chocolate' topic.

Writing a journal.

Clay work and painting.

Cooking stuff on a candle.

Making our own beach hut.

And intriguingly, *'Making toothpaste for an elephant.'*

Many of the memories that were listed included curriculum activities such as maths, sport, dance, music and drama. One 9-year-old child wrote: *'I have enjoyed art the most, because you can do what you want to and you can't get anything wrong.'* This is a tiny sample from two very different schools but I wonder what you recall, reading this, that is memorable about your own curriculum experience at school? What can we tell about the breadth of the curriculum, or lack of it, from children's SATs results? In many schools, the pressures of accountability have placed too much emphasis on attainment in English and maths at the expense of science, humanities and the arts.

Communities of learners

In Chapter 2, whole-school structures that facilitate pupil voice and democratic engagement were described. Within the curriculum at Wroxham these opportunities are extended through activities that encourage children to work with younger or older peers. The importance of being heard and being valued contributes significantly to children's confidence, self-knowledge and intrinsic motivation when they review their own learning. Music is taught throughout the school with specialist instrumentalists supporting the development of expertise in young musicians. Each year, summer concerts take place over two evenings, with packed programmes, as so many children wish to perform. Children who may only be able to play a few notes are accompanied by their teacher and applauded with warmth and genuine encouragement. Others may have been practising for several years and are able to play as part of a band or ensemble. Young people who left the school years earlier often return to join in with some of the pieces and parents are also invited to share in the performances. Two years ago, at one of the summer concerts, Louisa, from Year Six, gave a stunning performance of 'Czardas' by Vittorio Monti, accompanied by her violin teacher on the piano. Louisa comes from a family of musicians and practised her violin daily even when she went on a residential school trip. Her practice, dedication and passion for music inspired others around her. Within an environment where positive states of mind are fostered among children and adults, there is recognition that the actions of today can impact on the achievements of the future. Katie, also from Year Six, played the violin well that evening but clearly had admiration for Louisa and ambition for her own future success. Last month I heard that Katie had performed as part of a prestigious concert at her secondary school, having mastered 'Czardas' after years of determined practice and expert teaching. There is a positive energy of hope that comes from working within a community of learners that believes in 'transformability'. Katie's achievement is an example of what can be achieved when we work hard at learning as opposed to marvelling at 'talent' and assuming that skills are innate.

Making connections

Enabling children to make connections in their learning is key to developing understanding and intellectual capacity. When Norman Thomas, latterly HM Chief Inspector for Primary Education, was a primary headteacher, he recalls 9-year-old Jeremy bouncing up to him in the corridor saying: 'This school needs a museum.' Point taken, a museum was duly established by the children. This deceptively simple anecdote encapsulates the importance of listening, engaging children's interests and extending their learning through opportunities that otherwise may be lost.

One of the ways that we seek to embed learning at Wroxham is through offering genuine opportunities for children to explain their thinking, or to design presentations that consolidate learning. When a term's study on a particular aspect of the curriculum has been completed, a celebratory event is often organized that gives children a chance to share their learning. In Year Two, the class invited their parents to view their inventions at the end of a design and technology project. Year Three, after studying the Victorians, organized a Great Exhibition. Study of the Vikings in Year Five led to the establishment of a pop-up museum with many guides available to describe the artefacts exhibited. Self-assessment and critical evaluation from peers forms part of the process of reviewing what has been learned and inspires areas for further investigation.

At Wroxham, the curriculum is organized into termly themes, usually based on history, geography or science. However, there is also plenty of space for innovation and for opportunities to respond to new interests or ideas. Most recently, the school has become inspired to build more environmental awareness. All children take part in Forest School lessons every week and Wroxham has become an Open Futures school, aiming to help children and the wider community benefit from growing and cooking food. We now keep chickens and plan to plant crops on the field alongside our thatched Celtic hut. These developments to the curriculum emerge through a culture of co-agency between children, teachers and families.

Talking about mathematics

Luke Rolls, now teaching at the University of Cambridge Primary School, has a particular interest in supporting children to build their capacity for mathematical thinking. When interviewing children about mathematics at a previous school, Luke recorded the following advice to teachers from an 8-year-old child frustrated within a situation where he had not experienced agency: *'Maybe if you listen to the children's point of view, it will be easier for them.'* Luke believes that the classroom culture should provide opportunities where children *want* to contribute and build the confidence to do so: *'Children need to trust that their teacher won't be frustrated by their response, their peers won't laugh at them and that it will be worthwhile for them to offer their thoughts.'*

An overtly non-judgemental stance on the part of the teacher, who shows that he values individual student responses, has a subtle but powerful impact. When Luke asked 9-year-old Hanit what advice she would give to other teachers of mathematics, the first thing that came to her mind was a socio-emotional aspect of learning:

> *What I would say to teachers of maths? Try and make children feel comfortable. Before, I used to feel scared because I was worried if I had got the wrong answer. I think teachers need to make the children feel that it's OK if they get the wrong answer.*

Luke's view is that if children feel they might be 'put down' in however subtle a way in a class, it is unsurprising if they resist offering their ideas about what they understand, let alone sharing misconceptions. As discussed in Chapter 1, developing a culture of trust is of paramount importance. It is important to ensure that the ethos of the class is conducive to developing dialogue and co-agency. The opportunity to formatively assess learning is 'severely undermined' when dialogue is not abundant in our classrooms. Some children may have the necessary resilience to learn in an unforgiving learning environment but this is not to say they will be unaffected by it:

> *If my teacher is really strict, I still don't mind about making mistakes, but I do get kind of nervous.*

> (Hasnain, 8 years old)

> *Teach it a bit less strict and bit more fun because if it's too strict, children won't enjoy because it will get too much for them and that makes it harder for them to learn in other lessons, because they will be stressed.*

> (Jack, 9 years old)

When an emotionally safe environment is established, the children explain that it is their peers, rather than us, that become the expert teachers:

> *If teachers want their children to learn and not just write loads of stuff like a robot . . . if you want them to actually learn, children need to talk. Maybe a teacher can't explain it to a child but maybe a child can explain it to a child because children are weird in their own way . . . and they can understand each other better. When a child says it to another child, it makes sense to them.*

(Hanit, 9 years old)

Talking about numbers

Jo Boaler's most recent book *Mathematical Mindsets* (2016) offers a vitally important view of mathematics, which refutes the notion that there is a 'math gene' that means some people are 'naturally' able to understand this subject. She suggests (p. 267) the following messages should be given to all students of mathematics:

- everyone can learn math to the highest levels;
- mistakes are valuable;
- questions are really important;
- math is about creativity and making sense;
- math is about connections and communicating;
- math class is about learning not performing;
- depth is more important than speed.

In their Stanford *How to Learn Math* (Boaler 2013) online course, Cathy Humphreys and Jo Boaler introduce many classrooms around the world to the idea of 'dot talks'. These number talks are designed to communicate to pupils that the way they 'see' maths is valid and worthy. Rather than 'producing' an answer, they are given the chance to 'mathematize' about the posed representation themselves and express their ideas. It is the teacher's reaction that defines the value this activity is given in class. Luke Rolls emphasizes the difference that adopting a reflective, open approach to really listening to children's words and ideas has within the classroom:

> *When we stop cutting off conversations and really listen, pupils seem to follow suit and their ideas can be truly heard and responded to. As the dialogue develops, what often becomes evident is how pupils' perspectives can be surprisingly different within the class. This communicates an*

important aspect of learning maths; being open-minded and looking outwards. As students and as teachers, our perspectives do not limit us to that which we are already familiar with but open up possibilities of new ideas, new thinking and new understanding.

Luke explains that the work of Torrance and Pryor (2001) into convergent and divergent assessment helped him to develop his use of formative assessment. He realized that it was important for him to understand the difference between questions or instruction devised to capture whether children have understood something taught, as opposed to, or in conjunction with, assessment to see what children understand. The latter implies more open-ended tasks where there is not always a single answer and, through a mathematical context, we learn where individuals, groups and classes are flourishing and where instruction needs to move to next. We see this dialogic approach at work in Chapter 4 when we learn about inclusive maths mastery lessons being developed at Wroxham.

'Let's Think' through maths

It is often pointed out by mathematics educators that while mathematicians will spend prolonged periods of time on a problem, in maths lessons students are more commonly asked for a series of quick responses to closed-type question and answer problems. This goes beyond 'wait time'; it's about teachers' and students' co-construction of what maths is and how it should be learned. Maths lessons in the 'Let's Think' programme (www.letsthink.org.uk), which has its roots in cognitive acceleration, aim to turn classes away from discussions that resemble games of 'ping-pong' and towards those which more seem more like 'basketball', where there is a dynamic of passing, shooting and defence in dialogue *around* the class as opposed to back and forth to the teacher. In these lessons, teachers give students the opportunity to construct or reconstruct an understanding of some of the big ideas in maths.

The Giant's Palace

Luke describes a lesson that helped his Year Four class construct the relational aspect of place value. This was a 'Let's Think' lesson called 'The Giant's Palace' (Seleznyov 2009 – www.letsthink.org.uk/resource_folder/giants-palace/). In a 'Let's Think' lesson, there is no mention of a learning intention, success criteria or a specific maths topic. The lesson is introduced as a 'thinking lesson'. In Luke's classroom he started this episode of learning by beginning to read an adapted version of the story, 'How Big is a Foot?' The tale is of a tyrannous king who rules the land, demanding that his carpenter makes his wife a bed 6 feet long and 3 feet wide. The carpenter tries to make the bed, measuring with his small feet, and presents the king with a bed far too small for the queen. The king demands that from now on everything should be measured using his feet only. At this point, children go off and try this out, measuring things with a template of the king's foot, only to find that the measurements are crude and inaccurate. This finding mirrors that in the story where the king takes advice about finding a more precise sub-measurement. He learns from his counsel that 10 fairy feet are the same size as a king's foot. Children then try to measure some items with this new more accurate unit of measure, only to find again that it is still not precise enough to measure everything. To overcome this problem in the story, it is suggested to the king that pixie feet, of which 10 are equivalent to a fairy's foot, could be used to refine measurements further. The children's task is to discover a way to record their measurements. Through class dialogue, it becomes clear that longhand methods are very time consuming, and some children come up with shorthand versions (e.g. 3G2F4P). Depending on previous learning, some children will make a link to decimals and suggest using these. In the second episode of the lesson, children are asked to order a set of decimal numbers to which they relate the place value of the tenths and hundredths to the fairy and pixie feet and so bridge from their experiences of the concrete/pictorial to the abstract.

This sequence of events in the lesson is not however without confusion or disagreement. For example, when it comes to ordering the decimals, children will argue different perspectives and ideas. Dealing with cognitive conflict in the students is one of the real insights for teachers of the 'Let's Think' approach. Luke asked some of his Year Four children how they felt about this peculiarity of 'thinking lessons' where there may still be a lot of perplexity, questions and no clear answer to the posed problem at the end of a lesson: *'Well, it's kind of annoyingly good . . . At first, you don't know which way to go but at the end, you know your brain is growing, which is the good bit'* (Hanit, 9 years old).

> *It's like a good confusion because then next time you're going to know about that challenge. Just say as a metaphor . . . You're going, and then there's a wall ahead of you. What do you do? You can't go over or around it so you have to climb it. If you think, oh I can't do this, then you smash into the wall. So in order to do well, you have to know your way. You need to know how to get over the wall, not just try and go around it. Being confused before, helps you, because it lets you know the next time that you need to climb the wall and not smash into it.*

(Jack, 9 years old)

Dialogue inspired by cognitive conflict

If we are used to plenaries as tight assessment opportunities from which we can plan our next day's lesson, we may find ourselves uncomfortable with the idea of so much uncertainty at the end of a lesson. Cognitive conflict, that is genuinely being challenged and puzzled by a problem, sets off a process where learners actively seek equilibrium – a reordering of their thinking that can accommodate a new piece of information about the world. An image to describe this is similar to the settling of liquid in a container after it has been shaken. Assessment of learning in lessons such as this is often unquantifiable in the moment. Through the rich talk in our classes, however, we can assess who is claiming a misconception as fact, and whether they are becoming increasingly confident or self-questioning in their position.

Avoiding robotic maths

Some adults can quote the formula for the area of a circle: 'Pi-r-squared'. However, being able to recite this phrase does not necessarily imply understanding; this lies in their construction of the concept, which, in turn, is achieved through experience and by questioning what that experience reveals. There are many concepts in maths that have been taught through puzzling traumas of trying to remember an impossible series of apparently meaningless procedures. The way many of us were taught maths as children was through rules like 'two minuses make a plus', which often leads to robotic calculation without understanding.

Using one of the many excellent NRich teacher guides (Gilderdale and Kiddle 2011) about teaching positives and negatives, alongside using a positive to negative number line, Luke's class looked at two models for calculating with negative and positive numbers. Children learned through playing an adapted version of the NRich dice game called 'Tug Harder', using the simple model of red and blue counters to understand why two positive blue counters and two red negative counters can cancel each other out. Children enjoy using manipulatives in lessons like these; they help them not only to solve the maths problem presented but also to understand the structural relations of the maths involved. When children join Luke's class, they sometimes tell him that in previous classes they were not given access to maths resources, something they feel is a powerful aid to their learning:

> If you don't have resources, if you just do it in your mind, the person will try to work it out but completely forget what they were working on. If you have things in front of you like the Dienes blocks, and you can see, say, the two hundred, it is easier and more fun for children to do it. The teachers will see that it is more enjoyable for the students to do and so they will keep wanting to use it.
>
> (Gilly, 9 years old)

In working with manipulatives as Luke did in the negative numbers lesson, children are challenged by different aspects of learning. Some find the language reasoning structures more difficult: 'positive four subtract six, equals negative two', others question whether they are subtracting negative numbers and if so what would happen. Some children in the lesson move onto relating number facts and recognizing number triads. With careful task design, all children can work within a context where the ceiling is high enough that they will not be limited. Formative assessment here links with the teacher's subject and pedagogical content knowledge. If the teacher is clear about what the maths in the task is, he is increasingly able to anticipate the difficulties children might encounter while bearing Natasha's advice in mind: *'If a child needs help, don't help them too much so that they get the answer, just give them a hint'* (Natasha, 9 years old).

Asking questions and questioning answers

Mike Ollerton, a freelance mathematics consultant, recalls a lesson he taught while a secondary teacher, where effective learning occurred as a result of students questioning what he had previously told them. The example is from a lesson with a Year Nine group, and is about two pupils asking: *'Can you show us how to do long division?'*

The lesson was based upon an exploration of fractions as decimals; one task required students to produce a two-way division table on a 2 cm square-dot grid. Using calculators, Mike asked students to do just enough calculations to be able to see patterns and then predict further results. This prompted a variety of discussion, some of which centred on the notion of recurring decimals. Katy and Jane were exploring recurring decimal values of sevenths and Mike told them the 'final' 1 on their calculator display of 0.1428571 was the beginning of a recurring sequence. He realized subsequently that this was an example of unthinkingly telling children something and expecting them to accept the answer. Fortunately, not all students allow this to go unchecked and here was a case in point. The girls were not satisfied with what their teacher had told them and after a short while asked Mike how *he* knew, or how *they* could know that the final 1 on the calculator display was the first digit of a recurring sequence.

Pleased that Katy and Jane showed motivation to want to know, Mike was nevertheless conscious that anything other than a lengthy explanation might leave them feeling less confident of understanding the process. He then attempted to show them how to do long division, however his explanations were unclear and they were unable to understand. After further confusion, they decided to look at 'easier' fractions with denominators of 5, 10 and 20.

Again, Mike realized that his explanations had been inadequate. He had told them a procedure but to them it had been meaningless – an example of the kind of 'robotic' maths discussed earlier. Sadly, many pupils would have given up at this point; however Katy and Jane were persistent. A few minutes later they returned again asking: 'Can you show us again how to do long division?' Mike went through further calculations slowly and carefully and, after a while, they both declared they could understand the process and confirmed this by carrying out some similar calculations.

Here the students' motivation had provided Mike with the impetus to explain a mechanistic procedure more clearly. A significant factor was their desire that he share his knowledge; they recognized a need and signalled a preparedness to gain the knowledge they wanted. Such preparedness grew, in part, from the types of problems Mike offered: 'The motivation to master new problems is most likely to spring from having enjoyed the satisfaction of finding solutions to problems in the past' (von Glasersfeld 1995: 181).

Some moments later, another student, Nicola, asked if it would be a good idea to extend the grid into the other three quadrants. Her question opened up other possibilities which Mike hadn't planned for. This idea, which was entirely of Nicola's volition, showed her independence of thought and her developing understanding of the interconnected nature of mathematics. She was, therefore, able to relate concepts in a present context to learning experiences from previous contexts: '. . . real learning, seems to be more a matter of seeing a question than learning an answer' (Sotto 1994: 7).

Nicola's question provided the basis for conversations about:

- fractions and decimals in all four quadrants;
- how the gradients of the lines previously drawn in the positive quadrant extend into the third (−x, −y) quadrant;
- the effect of dividing a negative number by a negative number.

In just one lesson within the context of learning about fractions and decimals, students engaged not just with the ideas their teacher had asked them to think about, but showed initiative to extend their thinking, ask questions and, in turn, gain ownership of the mathematics. Such events endorse a view of mathematics as a multitude of interconnected ideas, the synthesis of which develops a wider understanding of the world.

Alex, a Year Five child from Wroxham, offers a similar insight when he sums up the need for a meaningful curriculum:

> You need to understand the concept of what you are doing. If you just get the answer and you don't really know what you are doing, then you haven't really worked it out. You need to usually get the answer and get the concept of it, so you know what you have done and how to do it and then you know the question.

(Alex, 10 years old)

Connecting with Shakespeare

For a number of years, Jackie has been including the study of a Shakespearian play as part of the curriculum for 8- and 9-year-olds. When she first proposed this in her previous school, she experienced scepticism from her headteacher. She felt he was 'condescending' about her children's capacity to connect meaningfully with Shakespearian literature, claiming that they would 'lack the maturity to understand, read or respond to such material at the age of eight and nine years'. Undeterred, Jackie provided each child in her class with their own copy of *A Midsummer Night's Dream*.

> *I find that once children know the basic story, not only do ALL children find interacting with the language exciting and illuminating, they all participate at the same 'entry level' so that, contrary to popular opinion, every child can access and find meaning in this challenging but shared and safe context.*

Study of Shakespeare in Jackie's classroom provides children with another platform to develop their sense of self-discovery, personal learning tools and empowerment:

> *The real value in the study of the plays is in the rich discussion surrounding characters' motives, actions and themes. I have never ceased to be amazed by the depth at which the Year Four children in my class are able to discuss key aspects as well to spot connections that I have missed.*

Danny, a 9-year-old boy in Jackie's class, presented as 'an angry frustrated child with ADHD with low levels both of concentration and achievement to date and a high level of self-doubt'. His favourite refrain in task avoidance was to declare, *'[I] didn't get it* [because] *I'm stupid'*. Jackie's headteacher, nervous about whole-class teaching of Shakespeare, called her to a meeting. He declared that she should reinstate 'ability' grouping in her class in line with the practice of other year groups at the school. He declared that he felt it was inappropriate for someone of Danny's 'ability' to have to 'struggle through' such content. Not only was this inaccurate, it made huge prejudgements of Danny:

> *In fact, Danny, just as though he was watching soap on TV, made hugely insightful comments about character action and consequence, the whole way through our study. He and others responded wholeheartedly to the strategies I used to bring the play and the original writing to life. I believed that all the children would understand and connect meaningfully with the play and they did.*

Danny was able to amaze the headteacher on his next classroom visit with his ease around the original text, his capacity to decode meaning and his strong views on character action. The headteacher's surprise was such that he suggested that other teachers come to observe the children and what they were capable of comprehending and analysing. Jackie's example illustrates the importance of creating a classroom climate where genuine dialogue and debate is given space and where children are trusted to challenge themselves and engage with ideas. Had she approached the teaching of Shakespeare with anticipation that many in the class may not be able to access or understand the text, it is likely that her expectations would have been met.

The joy of making language accessible

St Helen's School in Ipswich has a high intake of children with English as an additional language. As we have seen in this chapter, capacity to engage in language to support learning is a vital part of a *Learning without Limits* culture. Headteacher Clare Flintoff has developed, with her staff team, an approach to enhancing communication skills that builds upon the Progression in Language Structures developed by Tower Hamlets EMA Team in London in 2009. Each language structure has a linked animal; children soon start describing with chameleon language, comparing with zebra language and deducing with bat language. Simply knowing that the sentence might start with a phrase such as: 'On the one hand . . .' empowers writers and speakers of all kinds to decide what comes next. Clare says that children at St Helen's are given 'a voice' and they no longer say, 'I don't know what to write.'

Children at St Helen's helped to match each language function with 12 different animals. These form attractive prompts around the school:

Language of opinion: lion

The lion is the king of the jungle and thinks his opinion is very important.

Language of retelling: elephant

With it's famous long memory, the elephant can recall past events in detail.

Language of hypothesis: turtle

A hypothesis is an explanation made on the basis of limited evidence as a starting point for further investigation. The turtle will hide in its shell to gather evidence before coming out for further investigation.

Language of argument: shark

It cuts through the water, without swerving or being swayed by others' opinions. It takes on board alternative ideas and positions but, ultimately, holds its line.

Language of prediction: giraffe

The giraffe is very tall and can see what is coming which helps him or her to predict events.

Language of comparison: zebra

The zebra has black and white stripes and no two zebras are the same.

Language of mathematical explanation: bee

Bees are systematic, logical workers. They are organized and efficient. Bees break down complex processes into individual steps.

Language of explanation: dolphin

The dolphin has very advanced communication skills.

Language of sequencing: octopus

Sequencing places things in order. The octopus has eight legs, which it has to keep in order. The octopus has three hearts, a first, a second and a third.

Language of deduction: bat

Bats fly in the dark, without trouble, and they have a very good detection system to do this. They use clues from their surroundings.

Language of description: chameleon

The chameleon can sometimes copy its surroundings and changes colour depending on its mood. Describing is making a copy of something or representing something. There are many ways to describe a chameleon.

Language of evaluation: tree frog

The tree frog evaluates which branches to climb on by testing them first and deciding which grip to use.

(www.sthelensprimary.net)

At St Helen's, teachers explain that the tool of 'language structures' might be usefully imagined through a comparison with drama and the stage. The structures, the particular learned phrases, sentence beginnings and sentence structures provide the platform for what may be written or said – the stage as it were. While on stage, knowing and feeling happy with its parameters, pupils develop the 'drama' of their writing. The children at St Helen's are convinced that deploying different forms of language structures helps them to express their spoken and written ideas more powerfully:

In my opinion, language structures helped me get a Level 4 in writing. They substitute boring sentence starts and are like a flashlight. You can turn the light on at any time and in any subject. As my first languages are Bengali and Arabic, they have really helped me with my third language.

(Year Six child)

Jose, 10 years old, wanted to write about footballer Fernando Torres. Here is his first draft: *'Fernando Torres plays for Chelsea. He is fast. I think he scored the winning penalty. He has a tattoo. He is a talented player. I think he is a top scorer.'* This is Jose's revised draft, written one week later:

I would like to argue that Fernando Torres is a key player in world football. Opponents may argue that there are more important players all round but I assert that Torres shows more individual skill and reaches speed more quickly than most. Evidence tells us that he has scored nine goals this season, even though he has been injured. Indeed, he is a positive role model and ran the London Marathon for charity. For this, he gains wider respect.

It could be said that much of this writing lacks nuance and maturity but the language structures serve as a tool for future fluency and the school community is convinced of the importance of giving children a confident voice. There are colourful displays throughout the school reminding children of the 12 animals and their corresponding language characteristics. Key words, phrases and prompts for each language structure are available in classrooms on word mats, laminated key cards and wall displays. Clare Flintoff and her team are passionate about the success of this approach, which they believe gives the children at St Helen's an opportunity to converse and communicate with confidence and articulacy.

In Years Five and Six the children perform a play by Shakespeare. Photographs of previous productions are proudly displayed throughout the school. While rehearsing at the end of the summer term, some of the girls gathered together to write about their school, in response to a request from their headteacher who wanted their opinions for this book. Here is the result of the girls' collaborative writing:

We know what we are, but know not what we may be.

Shakespeare, Hamlet

Where do we start? Schools are future-makers. Our ambition and morality shown by our dedicated staff has a symmetrical reflection on our exceptionally hardworking students. At its growing brain, St Helen's is always developing. Every minute counts. If you want every pupil to succeed in their dreams; every heart is needed.

Learning choices

Comfort is one thing that teachers prioritize. They, while trying to push our levels, make sure that we are comfortable with what we are doing. To be able to achieve this, our teachers set different levels in lessons so our pupils feel safer, calmer and not pressured.

Our students have their own opinion on how they prefer to learn. Some like to have set paragraphs – others choose to write completely freely. In maths children like to choose their level to feel free and happy about being able to do the maths.

Freedom: be the best you can be

Many schools say 'Sky's the limit' – we say 'There is no limit!' In this work-worthy school, we don't mind who we are. We do, however, think ahead about what we want to be when we're older. If you go to St Helen's, being the best you can be, looking up at your aspirations, there is no limit. We believe that we are one and, as one, we need to work to BTBYCB (our school motto, it means Be The Best You Can Be). To give us all a kick-start, along with many other events, St Helen's went to Ipswich Regent to hear Jo Mersh's story. This was hugely inspiring for all of us; many people now know how to pursue their dreams.

Behaviour

Behaviour at this school is by no stretch perfect. Despite this, teachers do notice a definite improvement in attitude, during the students' time at St Helen's. Children at this school are mostly quiet when they need to be, but enjoy school at the same time – this is the perfect combination. Sometimes our pupils get excited and that causes them to become a little bit silly (what child doesn't occasionally?)

The building

One crucial part of an 'excellent' school is the atmosphere; children have an encouraging spirit towards learning. In lessons we encourage our pupils to have a learning buzz – not the level of playground talking, just background noise about what they're learning. Whispering quietly, learning doesn't only happen in lessons. Learning can happen during playtimes and lunch-times as well. The feeling of our school is care; every teacher cares for every student. If we have a worry, any member of staff will be happy to help. This is one of the most important parts of school life.

Outside

Another important element of school life is the playtimes between lessons – not only do the children get to relax, it gives the teachers and other staff time to make and revise lesson plans. During play, children have an opportunity to enjoy our play equipment; it is very safe and no children have been injured. There is a rota for the play equipment so no injuries should happen. Having a rota means only one class is on the play equipment at a time, which increases safety.

Structures for our writing

Writing in our school is developing because all of our wonderful staff have provided us with the resources we have been utilizing to progress. These include: language structures (they help us start our sentences when we get writers' block), dictionaries, thesauruses and many other utensils that they have given us to improve. Some children find that having a blank piece of paper in front of them is most useful, whereas others prefer to have a set structure. All in all, everyone has their own way of learning.

Overall, St Helen's is one of the most pupil friendly, encouraging and accepting schools you will ever hear about. It is a mosaic, simple, yet complicated.

It is not in the stars to hold our destiny, but in ourselves.

Shakespeare, Julius Caesar

(Alice, Chloe, Rachel and Felicity)

The composition of this writing is quite consciously stylized and successfully demands impact. What we see here is the joy of playing with language for effect. We can imagine the girls trying out phrases, looking for quotes, juxtaposing words, squealing with delight when clever phraseology is rehearsed and agreed. These skilful writers know that they are deliberately using intricate building blocks to make each point and we can feel that they enjoy every moment. The writers' collective ambition to impress the reader about their wonderful school is never in doubt for a moment. If the use of techniques such as language structures can enable this kind of confidence among children learning English, it is truly a means to enhance equality.

Summary

The chapter began with a reminder of the importance of maintaining both breadth and quality across the entire curriculum. A curriculum that engages learners will be significantly enhanced when children's thinking and their capacity to learn are valued. Examples particularly within the context of mathematics teaching have been provided to illustrate how learning can be significantly enhanced through dialogue, thereby building capacity for understanding and enabling new cognitive connections to be made. When dialogic pedagogy is enabled within an expertly taught curriculum, children have the best possible chance of exceeding our expectations.

Next we consider ways in which classrooms can be organized without the limiting notion of fixed 'ability', thereby building on the opportunities that trust, inclusive pedagogy and an irresistible curriculum provide.

4

Beyond differentiation: Avoiding labelling

We can push our knowledge to a higher level. I like picking my own challenges because I can give myself a step forward.

(Oscar, 11 years old)

Differentiation has been a routine part of English classroom practice for many years. However, this approach has unintentionally set a 'ceiling' on the learning of some children. The thinking behind differentiation is that children need to be supported in their learning and that within any class there will be a variety of starting points from children at different stages in their learning. The problem occurs when false, limiting assumptions are made about children's capacity to learn. Practice such as 'ability' grouping is often based on the premise that intelligence is fixed and that future attainment can be predetermined. The growth in the number of teaching assistants may also have accentuated a tendency towards increased 'learned helplessness' among many children. Hattie (2009), Webster et al. (2015) and Rowland (2015) raise an important challenge to the role that is often allocated to teaching assistants within primary classrooms.

Differentiation usually results in classroom organization with children sitting in fixed groups, where tasks of varying complexity are allocated according to preconceived assumptions about what children are capable of learning. Susan Hart (1998) flagged issues about the 'sorry tail' of differentiation and subsequently these arguments were explored in depth in *Learning without Limits* (Hart et al. 2004). Only recently has wider recognition been given to the unintended outcomes of 'ability' grouping. This chapter offers practical alternatives. In *Creating Learning without Limits* (Swann et al. 2012) we discussed the importance of refusing to see children's future learning as predictable or inevitable and described the liberating practice of 'choice and challenge' developed at Wroxham. Instead of subscribing to an orthodoxy that requires children to be grouped according to perceived attainment levels, some schools have been inspired to develop positive alternatives to 'ability' grouping, thereby enabling children to experience a sense of agency about their learning capacity.

As a means of ensuring that no child is limited in their learning, teachers may offer children a choice of task within lessons. This is a pedagogical strategy that comes from a central belief that listening to children matters. These teachers are keen to encourage children to build intrinsic motivation to challenge themselves in their learning, rather than passively waiting for others to judge their performance. The schools featured in this chapter offer an inclusive culture that avoids ranking and enables children to surprise them by what they can achieve. Children are highly motivated by working in this way as John, 10 years old, observed:

> *If you are challenging yourself and learning, it doesn't matter whether you are doing Challenge 1 all the time. It's what you think you are good at. You don't need to be at the top. If you're doing Challenge 1 it doesn't mean you are bad at maths, it just means you may not understand what you are doing in that lesson.*

(John, 10 years old)

How can I organize my classroom without 'ability' groups?

The Early Years Foundation Stage provides children with the skills they need to learn together within a class community. Building self-regulation, making decisions, negotiating with peers and developing the language of learning are all central to an Early Years ethos that promotes discovery and inquiry. In the schools featured here, there is a natural transition between the Foundation Stage and Year One. Building independence and self-knowledge is at the heart of an approach to assessment that seeks to engage the learner as an active participant in the process. From the earliest days in school, teachers who eschew limiting notions of fixed ability use the language of challenge throughout the curriculum, whether teaching physical education, supervising the building of dens in Forest School or teaching writing. Schools that embody the disposition of openness draw on a relentless determination to 'find a way through' for everyone. Teachers inspired by *Learning without Limits* find ways to enable every child to learn without ranking or labelling, while recognizing that within each class of 30 children there will be a considerable range of knowledge, skills and development. Some children may be very informed about the natural world and love talking about animals but find all forms of early writing difficult, others may be excited by numbers but dislike interacting with their peers, others may be reading fluently but fear speaking in front of others. Every teacher knows within minutes of meeting a class that there will be a delightful, complex mixture of characters with varying interests, passions and worries.

Instead of relying on data sheets and prior attainment grids as the first means of planning for learning, the teachers in this chapter use summative assessment data as a background metric. Their main energy is spent teaching lessons that create opportunities for children to engage within learning in a manner that is open to all, thereby creating high expectations of achievement from every child. Assessment in these schools has become a constant activity closely tied to an inclusive pedagogy that provides the necessary feedback teachers need, in order to refine, shape and extend the curriculum in response to the children's current understanding. For example, during a lesson the teacher may reveal a range of three progressively challenging questions on the screen and ask her class to select a question to answer using their individual whiteboards. In a classroom where learning is not limited, children are trusted to choose a question that challenges them because that is much more interesting than answering something robotically. When the class holds up their whiteboards to the teacher she is able to see at a glance how much the children have understood, thereby providing her with an instant assessment that can immediately inform her teaching.

When the children move to their tables to begin practising independently, they are often offered a choice of learning activities. Teachers help the children to make informed choices by briefly describing what each task involves, thereby assisting the process of self-assessment and enabling children to make an informed decision. The teacher may decide to continue working with children who have selected the simplest task or conversely may spend time extending the thinking of those who have chosen the most complex questions. This varies from class to class and depends on the content of the lesson, but it avoids dependency from some children who may quickly develop 'learned helplessness' seeking adult reassurance during every lesson. The aim is to free the children from notions of fixed 'ability' towards a notion of building learning capacity.

During independent work, the teacher may stop the children to share some responses to the task or to ask the children to self-assess using thumbs up (or down), reminding them that they can change their challenge if they feel they need to.

To further support children's understanding and independence, their work will often be marked by the teacher, sitting alongside them. Through questioning, the teacher is able to closely assess understanding to inform her planning for the next lesson. Children are encouraged to use self-assessment smiley, straight or sad faces at the end of their work. The teacher's feedback will often build on this, offering advice about next steps. If the child draws a sad face after attempting Challenge 3, the teacher may make a written comment suggesting trying Challenge 2 first in the next lesson. Conversely, a happy face may receive a prompt about trying a further challenge next time.

When planning and preparing lessons, teachers will typically prepare three progressively complex challenges with additional material ready if needed. Teachers recognize that every challenge should be presented as interesting and important. The aim is to replace a hierarchy of achievement comparing child against child with a culture of ambition and 'personal best'.

Sometimes, instead of choosing from a range of tasks, the teacher may plan an activity with colour-coded questions on each table. Children are thereby encouraged to go beyond the challenge they might usually choose and attempt other questions. This aims to keep opportunities open for every child to have a go at something they may usually avoid. There is a constant ongoing class dialogue about the importance of trying new things and thinking hard. At the end of each lesson teachers are careful to praise effort rather than attainment and to help the children see that they should be proud of trying their best. The message that learning is about achieving individual success is reinforced, reminding the class to resist any temptation to select the same challenges as their friends.

In some classes, each of the independent challenge tasks are is out on a 'challenge table', which allows the teacher to monitor the children's decisions and to remind everyone that should they find a task too easy or too hard they should move up or down accordingly. At Cherry Orchard School, Worcestershire, Year Five children took it in turns to run a 'help desk' within their classroom, where peers could come and describe what they were finding difficult. Often, the process of describing the problem aloud meant that as the child reread the task she could suddenly see what had been misunderstood. Alternatively, children were able to seek another task that would give them more opportunity to consolidate understanding before leaping forward again. The children's sense of control coupled with ambition to achieve is highly motivating. Evie (age 11), from Scole School in Norfolk, commented, *'Picking your challenge is a good idea because you can pick your level of difficulty and get smarter in stages.'*

Assessment of learning is considerably enhanced through dialogue. From the earliest days, children surrounded by others who listen carefully to them and prompt them gently with open questions will rapidly develop ways of explaining their thinking. At Banstead Infants, Surrey, children are taught to name different learning habits and become skilled at identifying these when describing their thinking as 'expert learners'. Inspired by the work of Guy Claxton (2002) the school devised eight 'habits of an expert' that the children use to evaluate their learning. The children are taught to be:

- adventurous;
- curious;
- observant;
- investigative;
- determined;
- imaginative;
- cooperative;
- reasoning.

They select the appropriate learning habits for the task – so, for example, the key habits of scientists could be described as being observant, curious and investigative underpinned by reasoning. In Years One and Two the children develop this further by explaining why a particular habit has been chosen and how it will improve the quality of their learning. For example, as writers the children may suggest that they need to be adventurous. They may then explain that an adventurous writer would be observant and imaginative while also including interesting vocabulary. Teachers at Banstead no longer write a daily timetable of what the children are 'doing' but rather what they will 'be': mathematicians, scientists, authors, gymnasts, computer scientists, artists, designers, musicians and so on. Stephanie Storrar, headteacher, says:

> *The result of the approach is that we have found that the children are analysing their learning more effectively; they know what they need to bring to learning and can evaluate to what extent they have used the habits to improve. Their self-esteem has improved as they see themselves as the experts. This confidence that they are capable and important learners results in the children having high expectations of what they can achieve.*

The emphasis in these classrooms is that children will develop the skill to explain their thinking. During class teaching, if a child offers an answer she may be asked to expand on her initial response and others may be asked to build on her ideas. Within subjects such as mathematics and science, misconceptions are uncovered when children are asked to explain their answers step by step. Immediate feedback may be gained through using whiteboards or number fans to help the teacher quickly gauge the collective understanding of the class. When the children are working independently, the teacher will often engage small groups or individuals in conversation to assess understanding and gain deeper insight into the children's reasoning. This also provides feedback that enables the teacher to scaffold learning through prompting or to extend as appropriate. At the end of the week the children may be asked to reflect on what they have understood from the topic that week, focusing on new learning and consolidation of previous learning. Open-ended investigative learning provides rich opportunities for formative assessment, which, used alongside low-stakes summative assessment, enables the teacher to build an informed picture of each child's developing understanding over time.

Recently, colleagues at Banstead have also introduced 'choice and challenge' to the curriculum, to enable their children to gain further independence and control over their learning. Stephanie Storrar says the children are now viewed as 'trusted partners' in the learning process.

What about progress? Can we really trust the children?

When 'choice and challenge' was first introduced into maths lessons at Banstead, teachers were worried about progress. Initially, a pedagogy of challenge and choice was introduced in mathematics, with children being offered four colour-coded levels of increasing difficulty or complexity. The children were told that they could move through the challenges during a session as they became more confident. This was difficult to start with, as the children did not understand the concept of challenge – for example, some chose the same challenge as their friend or they chose their favourite colour. The process needed lots of discussion and modelling to enable them to choose an appropriate challenge for them. As a result every session stopped five minutes early to discuss their choices.

Teachers were concerned that the children would only choose easy challenges but, with continued reinforcement of Dweck's (2012) growth mindset culture and modelling how to choose a challenge, the children began to surprise their teachers with the maturity of their choices. The approach that children took when selecting challenges was very revealing to their teachers. Often, girls, who were considered very capable mathematicians, chose an easier challenge than the teachers felt was appropriate, with the opposite being the case with the boys, many of whom went straight for the higher level challenges. The girls told their teachers that they preferred to practise to make sure they were confident before they moved on to the more difficult challenges. Many boys, however, said they were adventurous so decided to challenge themselves to see what they could do. The children began to understand themselves as learners and gradually became more skilled at selecting a challenge that would enable them to learn. Teachers at Banstead have found that being given choice has led to children thinking much more deeply about their learning, evaluating how and why they succeeded and how to move forward.

This comment is from a Reception child in the autumn term, having just been introduced to the concept of challenge: *'I chose to build with these bricks [Lego] because I haven't used them before and they are very small.'* From a Year Two child:

> *Some people don't choose the right challenge, why would they do that? I like to challenge myself. I have never done a green [starting level], sometimes I choose blue like when it is really tricky. Sometimes you can go straight to black or purple [mastery level]. If we choose a challenge that is too easy for us, then we are not learning. We need to choose a challenge that we get some right and some wrong. Making mistakes is learning.*

Giving children agency over choice of task gave the teachers insight into *how* the children were learning as well as *what* they were learning. Teachers found that by removing the limits to children's learning and offering them the choice of task, or leaving the task open-ended, the children surprised them and achieved far more highly than either they, or their teachers, might have expected. The use of challenge is beginning to spread to other subjects in this school and the children are using the concept of challenge in different ways to improve outcomes. They are extending their learning without teacher input:

> *When we were artists and we did [drew] parts of the school I did three drafts. The first one was good but it didn't fill the page and in the second*

one the roof was too small. Me and Billy we were working together and we were helping each other. Then we did a fourth draft and it was perfect, it looked 3D.

The introduction of 'choice and challenge' in many schools has led to greater self-evaluation by the children and has enabled teachers to gain a greater insight into how each child learns.

Transforming Year Five

Inspired by the national opportunity in England to review assessment practice, Lee Card, deputy headteacher, supported innovation among the Year Five teaching team at Cherry Orchard School, Worcestershire. One of the teachers there, Rebecca Thomas, led the development of a *Learning without Limits* approach in her Year Five group over the period of a year and explains her shock at the children's attitudes towards 'ability' at the beginning of Year Five before the team introduced a new way of working:

> *The first day the children were back we asked them what they thought of ability groups. The answers were astounding. The 'more able' loved it; they enjoyed being the 'bright' ones and having 'special' challenges set by the teacher. They also saw working with the teacher as a negative. The middle group were annoyed that they didn't get the same work and challenges as the other group; they wanted to try harder work but they had worked out they would never be moved up as there were only six seats on the top table. The 'less able' were affected the most. They felt 'dumb', useless, they thought they would never be allowed challenges as they usually work with the teaching assistant (some by Year Five were completely dependent on the teaching assistant to help them). This 'less able' group liked the sound of some of the challenges the top group had, but knew they would never get the chance.*

Astounded by the insights offered by the children at the beginning of Year Five, the teaching team decided to abandon all forms of 'ability' grouping immediately. This was a bold strategy given that sets remained in place in Years Four and Six. By the end of one year of trialling this approach, the Year Five team became passionate advocates for an inclusive pedagogy that trusts children to be experts about their own learning.

Strategies implemented across three classes in Year Five at Cherry Orchard School included:

- learning partners (changed weekly);
- introduction of 'choice and challenge';

- feedback dialogue in books between the child and teacher;
- class compliments books – for children to compliment others on their learning;
- use of 'hot' and 'cold' tasks;
- 'feelings': post-it notes were displayed at the beginning of new topic to enable everyone to recognize that new learning may feel risky; these were then reviewed after several weeks so that children could appreciate how their confidence and skill had grown;
- a 'help desk' was manned by children in the classroom;
- teaching assistants were deployed differently and were no longer attached to individual learners;
- the vocabulary of 'challenge' and a growth mindset was introduced.

The children were interested in the idea of growth and fixed mindset, as uncovered by Carol Dweck (2012) in her research. A neurosurgeon visited the school to talk to the children about the brain and neuroscience. They were inspired to think that they could learn more if they practised and rapidly began to enjoy liberation from 'ability' groups. The majority of children developed a new identity about themselves as learners, although a small minority of children who considered themselves 'gifted' found the new collaborative approach tiresome. Strategies such as engaging in a silent debate, a three-minute written debate on a shared piece of paper with several participants contributing connected ideas, enabled children to recognize that the 'loudest' children were not always the ones with the most original ideas.

Inspired by the work of Pie Corbett and Julia Strong (2011), the Year Five team implemented 'hot' and 'cold' tasks in order to reveal children's misconceptions and identify subsequent progress in their learning. Cold tasks were carried out on blue paper and were designed to show both the child and teacher what was already known and understood, in order that progress could be identified in subsequent lessons where 'hot' thinking could be demonstrated using flame-yellow paper. Once again we hear from Rebecca Thomas, Year Five teacher, who sums up the instant impact of this approach:

> The key was to get the children to evaluate their progress and to let them be in control of their learning and adjust tasks accordingly . . . It was amazing how much the children wanted to learn, when given the control to do so. Just as trust was bestowed upon us from senior management, we bestowed trust on the children – it worked brilliantly!

Peer learning

Vanessa Pearce at Beaudesert Lower School, Leighton Buzzard, recalls her earliest teaching experience that began to enlighten her about what could be possible in her classroom if she unleashed the children's ambition to be independent and explicitly showed them how to learn from each other.

When Vanessa became an Early Years leader she was keen to capitalize on the children's agency and energy for learning. Simple factors, like needing an adult to help with tying shoelaces, reduce the capacity of young children to be independent. Vanessa's response to this challenge was to teach a group of children in the class to be 'shoelace experts', each with the task of teaching others in the class. Pretty quickly, anyone with shoe difficulties knew there were children that would help them. This meant that movement between the classroom and outdoor learning area became much easier and freed Vanessa's time to observe and scaffold the children's play. As time progressed, Vanessa found she could help children to teach each other a wide range of practical tasks, such as how to add photographs and artwork to their learning journals and even to neatly double-mount their work for display in the class gallery. She realized that even very young children enjoy teaching others and can learn from their peers. She then introduced new maths and language games and activities that the children could learn and could teach to their peers:

> *I became aware of the power of children sharing learning with other children. My experience of teaching four- and five-year-olds taught me early on in my career that to underestimate a child would be one of the most limiting things that could happen to them.*

When starting school, whether primary or secondary, too many children risk being underestimated by their teachers. However, when the curriculum offers open-ended opportunities for children to problem-solve and think creatively, there is space for learners to show their new teachers the beginnings of what they are capable of.

Learning partners and paired working

Too often classrooms are organized into so-called ability groups to facilitate organizational management. At Wroxham, each class has a different approach to seating arrangements. The focus is always on achieving the optimum environment for learning, with children either choosing their own place to sit or choosing a learning partner to work with. In Years Five and Six, there is an expectation that children will change learning partners each week in order that they experience working alongside a variety of peers. The emphasis is on recognition that every child should aim to achieve their 'personal best' rather than working in competition or being ranked against others. The aim of learning partnerships and paired working is to provide constant opportunities for children to express their ideas and rehearse their thinking with a peer. Luke Rolls, from the University of Cambridge Primary School, interviewed some of his Year Four children from his previous school and asked them about pair work:

Partner and pair work helps you because if you don't know something, you can ask your partner and they might know it, and then you can discuss really well together. One person knows something and the other person doesn't so you work really well together and come to the same understanding.

(Jason, 8 years old)

Say I'm in a pair with someone and I explain it my way. Then I look at it a different way, from a different view from how they've explaining it and then I think 'yeah that's right, I can't believe I made that silly mistake'. Now I think about what I was thinking then and then I compare it to what I was thinking and then I imagine it in my head as two whiteboards, I misplaced this number, for example.

(Gabbie, 9 years old)

Ibrahim, also from Year Four, commented: *'My partner explained it to me and then it made me think more deeply.'*

Inclusive maths mastery

Building on the pedagogy of 'choice and challenge', which has been in place for over a decade at Wroxham, Sally Barker, the Year Six teacher at Wroxham, visited Shanghai recently to find out about a 'mastery' approach to mathematics. She was impressed by the Shanghai children's knowledge and confidence and set about trying to build on the best of what she had observed, while maintaining a *Learning without Limits* ethos within her classroom. A typical mathematics lesson now begins with a 10-minute instant recall activity, 'Magic Ten', which she uses to help the children recite multiplication facts, prime numbers, squared numbers and so on. This daily practice allows children to apply the basic facts they have learned to a variety of calculations. She reminds the children, 'If I know this . . . what else do I know?' The aim is to spot the relationship between the numbers in the calculation and the known facts, thereby allowing them to work more efficiently. For example, $0.07 \times 80 = 5.6$ (basic fact: $7 \times 8 = 56$, one factor has been divided by 100, the other has been multiplied by 10, and therefore the product must be divided by 10).

The majority of time in each lesson is led by Sally from the front of the class, with all children joining in and working through examples together. Typically, Sally starts by recapping an aspect of the previous lesson so that everyone feels confident about what is coming next. She then puts a question to the children and they think about how they could answer it themselves. This may involve them writing down a calculation in their book or studying a series of numbers to spot patterns, for example. The next stage is for everyone to share their thinking with their learning partner. Sometimes children will have the same answer and discuss how they arrived at that solution, other times children will differ in their approaches and may choose to use a green pen to edit their calculation. This enables children who may not have come up with an idea themselves to share in their learning partner's thinking and, if called upon, they will have the opportunity to articulate their new understanding to the rest of the class. This model enables every child to describe the process they have undergone, thereby building metacognition and consolidating learning. It is an empowering model for those children who may work more slowly but can nevertheless understand what their partner tells them. Sally then chooses a volunteer member of the class to work through the calculation for the class. As the process is described, Sally presents this on the screen and annotates as the child articulates each stage, requesting that the child explain how she knows what to do next. It would not be acceptable, for example, for a child to say, 'I knew I had to add a nought' – an explanation demonstrating understanding of place value would be expected. Effectively, this process what Alexander (2008) describes as 'dialogic teaching'. This builds upon the ethos of listening and co-agency that is developed throughout the school from the earliest days in the Foundation Stage. The climate of trust and openness within the class means that children are confident about sharing their thinking both within a learning partnership and with the whole class, as it is the *thinking*, rather than existing prior knowledge, that is celebrated. This often means that almost the whole class is able to volunteer to share, thereby building the confidence of the majority.

If a child begins to talk through their example to the class and a misconception is revealed, this provides a valuable teaching opportunity. If, for example, a child were to say that when multiplying fractions both the numerators and denominators had to be multiplied but could not explain why this should be the case, it would provide an opportunity for further teaching to the whole class. In this instance the teacher may ask: 'But why?' and if the child is unable to answer, the teacher can offer this back to the class saying, 'Let's explore why we do this' or maybe, 'Can anyone else explain to us why we would multiply both the top and the bottom of a fraction?' If no one is able to explain to the class, the teacher has identified a misunderstanding that may not otherwise have come to light in the rule-bound maths that we encountered in Chapter 3 where children follow processes and instructions because they have learned the method without understanding it. Sally's dialogic approach within an otherwise formally structured lesson allows *every* child to engage with learning.

The class teaching is very much a collaborative approach, with discussion about how to reach answers, what to do and why. Different ways of approaching mathematics are used, often offering visual, concrete and abstract examples. As the main class teaching progresses, Sally introduces what she calls an 'assessment for learning' (AfL) question. At this point, the children work through an example of the new learning covered earlier in the lesson. They know that they are expected to work totally independently and are given two to three minutes to work through a question, doing something that has just been taught but using different numbers, to see if they can do this on their own. The children write this down in their book as an AfL question, showing all of their workings. Once they have done this, they share their answer with their learning partner. This whole process only takes a few minutes but enables both the child and the teacher to see who has understood and who is still working towards understanding. At this stage in the lesson, the children move to individual practice for the final 20 minutes. Children who self-assess that they can work individually on the basis of their AfL question will work through up to 12 questions prepared by the teacher. Questions written by the teacher are designed to be accessible to every child and, through variation, to embed the skills taught during the lesson. Every child in the class works through the same questions, which begin simply and become progressively more complex. Children who may still be unsure will work through the same questions but will join a guided practice group facilitated by the teacher. If children are working independently but seek help, they display a blue card while attempting a different question. This simple system flags to the teaching assistant that help is needed, without a child wasting time by putting their hand up to signal for assistance. Children who join the guided practice group will not be the same children every lesson, as they self-select on the basis of their understanding that day. This is the skill that has been developed throughout the school using the choice and challenge approach described earlier. Children who initially join the guided practice group may only stay for a short while and then return to their usual seat to continue independently.

The idea is to present a particular type of mathematics through variation in as many formats as possible, some of which will be quite straightforward, with others that are increasingly complex. In the past, four or five challenges may have been offered by Sally within her Year Six class. In this new way of working, the majority of time has switched from individual practice to collaborative class teaching. Within each daily set of questions, the first few will be from what historically would have been Challenge 1; for many children they are able to reel these off in a matter of minutes and move on. Some children will be able to complete all 10 to 12 questions within the time available. The lesson is typically an hour and 10 minutes but is full of activity, checking understanding and collaboration. When the children talked about maths in their learning review meetings this year, they all spoke excitedly about their lessons and how much they felt they were learning. Similarly, Sally is equally inspired by her new approach to building learning capacity: *'The more you question yourself as a teacher, the more confident you become and the more you learn.'*

A whole-school approach

Scole School is a small rural school in Norfolk. The headteacher, Mark Carlyle, decided to implement 'challenge and choice' at this school two years ago. This meant moving away from 'ability' groups to enabling much more freedom for the children to self-select tasks within lessons. He interviewed Year Six children at the end of their time at Scole and asked them to reflect on this new approach. The children were able to recall previous practice of being grouped according to perceived 'ability' and were able to contrast this experience with freedom to choose. Several of the children refer to the kindness of their teachers and the support that they offer:

> *We are pushed, not in a way that we feel pressured but in a way so we can reach our potential. The teachers are patient, kind and they encourage progress and learning. We are given many opportunities to progress and choose our challenges, which is very effective.*

(Nathan, 11 years old)

> *Teachers care about you and help you if you are stuck by giving a little hint but they have high expectations. One thing I value is that everyone knows you, knows what you're like and who you are . . . I think that choosing your challenges is a great idea because then you could choose what you still need to work on.*

(Dan, 10 years old)

The children are very clear about the importance of learning within a culture of high expectations:

> *Scole has high expectations for everyone. Being able to choose your challenge allows you to push your abilities to the limit but also allows students to pick a challenge which is not too hard or easy for them.*

(Daisy, 11 years old)

> *Learning at Scole is very helpful because we have challenges that match everyone's individual abilities. The teachers never stop encouraging us, which in my opinion makes us independent and much more confident. It makes us appreciate teachers more because they care about our learning and improvements.*

(Anne, 11 years old)

The culture of the school is clearly a combination of aiming to achieve high standards but within an emotionally secure and enabling environment. Carl (10 years old) sums this up with his comment: *'I like the learning here because there's always a level of work to suit you.'*

Throughout this chapter we have seen the impact of children (and teachers) being encouraged to lift limits on their learning by trying new things. Contrast this with a story told to me by a conference delegate recently, remembering her son's experience of primary school. She recalled that on one occasion he came home, very crestfallen, having been reprimanded sharply by his teacher for turning the page in his textbook and carrying on with some calculations. His teacher had reportedly snapped furiously: *'You are a very naughty boy. I was saving those sums for tomorrow!'*

Summary

This chapter began with a reminder about the unintentional limiting impact of the practice of differentiation and has offered examples of alternative practice. Alternatives to 'ability' grouping include 'choice and challenge' and whole-class teaching that avoids ranking. The benefits for young children of linking their learning behaviours to 'expert' traits was also explored.

Children's agency and confidence about learning appears to shine through when the classroom is a place where it is safe to take risks and aim for self-improvement. It is also evident that teachers' efficacy and self-worth is enhanced within such classrooms. Another way of seeing learning and assessment becomes possible within a culture of trust, where inclusive pedagogy and a meaningful curriculum enable children to reveal both their misconceptions and their depth of understanding. In the next chapter we consider children's writing, including a section written by Michael Armstrong that offers another way of assessing the quality of children's writing.

5

Assessing writing

In our concern for the predetermined standard we miss the value of the individual work.

(Professor Michael Armstrong)

Assessing writing

This chapter focuses on children's writing and emphasizes the importance of valuing children's written words as a means to celebrate and understand their thinking and imagination. We begin with analysis of writing and feedback from the Year Six class of 10- and 11-year-olds at Wroxham. This is the standard form of 'apprentice'-style teaching whereby children attempt to refine their skills as a writer, following explanation, modelling and feedback from the teacher. This is how writing is taught and assessed in the vast majority of schools, although the examples provided illustrate the *quality* of writing achieved within an inclusive environment of co-agency and trust.

Michael Armstrong, an advocate for *Learning without Limits* contributes a summary of a powerful group analysis of an illustrated story, *The Gingerbread Place* by Ceva, a seven-year-old author. His analysis examines how we might consider alternative ways of appreciating and assessing the literary intent of young writers. Finally, we move away from school altogether and delight in one child's independent illustrated writing completed at home, purely for the love of it.

Feedback to apprentice Year Six writers

Studying examples of writing from the Year Six class at Wroxham, this section considers ways in which it is possible to celebrate and value children's writing while also supporting further development, through detailed feedback.

We first met Polly in Chapter 2, where we discovered that during her first years in school she found most aspects of English very difficult. For the following piece of writing, completed when she was 10 years old, Polly chose a photograph of a hooded person on a snowy railway platform as the stimulus for a descriptive passage:

> *Her face is destroyed, she slouches her body, holding only a few bags. There, she stood, looking at the train, slowing pasting by. Her face kept a frown. She had freezing cold shaking hands red as bold as a poppy. She felt distraught. The train gradually disappeared into the distance.*

> *Her emotions struck her, a tear lightly slid down her frowned face. She felt lonely, sad and upset. She stood there in her small thin layer coat, freezing cold shivering.*

> *She continuously stood there hour after hour. She patiently waits, for the next echoing sound of the train. Repeating itself over and over again.*

This is Polly's final draft. She received verbal feedback from her teacher and her peers during the writing process and was given some top line written feedback but it is the final draft that her teacher uses to provide a detailed written response:

> *Polly, this is a very moving description, it is so beautifully crafted, well done.*

> *I love your choice of descriptive language, every sentence seems to contain yet another word to describe her despair. You have also incorporated a wonderful simile to describe her frozen hands 'as bold as a poppy'.*

> *Not only have you used some wonderful language, you have also managed to spell almost every word correctly. Your punctuation is also largely secure and you have used paragraphs to organize your ideas well.*

> *Next steps:*

> * *Make sure you stay in the same tense throughout – use the edit to check this.*
> * *Remember to use commas to separate all lists of adjectives.*

We could add that Polly's use of phrases such as 'her face kept a frown', 'pasting by' and 'frowned face' add a poetic use of language that has considerable impact on the reader. The combination of encouragement from the teacher and detailed advice about improvement of technical skills enables children to use the teacher's response to good effect in their next piece of writing. This is not vague praise of the 'well done' variety, but feedback about the success of the writer's engagement with the task, followed by specific areas for development.

In another series of lessons, the teacher introduced the idea of metaphor and imagery and asked the children to write poems about themselves. The first piece that we examine is by 10-year-old Ned:

> *I'm usually as happy as a dog*
>
> *When I'm hyper I'm as hyper as thunder and lightening*
>
> *I'm as hyper as a fizzy drink,*
>
> *Popping up and down.*

Ned is a child who finds sitting still almost impossible. His poem bounces around the page in a manner that reminds us of the poet. Nevertheless, his teacher's feedback is thorough and values Ned's contribution:

> *Ned you have chosen three good similes to describe your personality, I particularly like the comparison to thunder and lightning. Your punctuation is good throughout, although you need to read your poem aloud to check where you need a comma.*
>
> *Next steps:*
>
> - *You need to practise joining your handwriting.*
> - *You were asked to include a metaphor too. Could you have removed 'as' to turn a simile into a metaphor?*

Attempting the same task, 10-year-old Charles' poem demonstrates the wide variety of responses in a class that may emerge from an open-ended task:

> *I am a glue stick.*
>
> *Stuck as can be,*
>
> *I'm like a garage*
>
> *He's as tyrered as me,*
>
> *I'm so sarcastic,*
>
> *As you can tell*

A bright spark,

A ringing bell

I am a wizard,

A master with words

I'm like a plane

As high as the birds

I am a tear drop

The start of a cry

An open door,

So; who am I?

The teacher's response illustrates her own subject knowledge as a means of enabling 10-year-old Charles to improve his work still further:

> *Wonderful work Charles. You are so right to say that you are a master with words, you have certainly crafted a very effective poem here. What I liked about it most is that your sense of humour permeates your writing.*
>
> *I particularly like the metaphor of a tear drop and the clever way that you develop this idea. You have presented your work very well, your spellings are all secure as is your punctuation.*
>
> *Next steps:*
>
> * *I would now like you to really focus on the rhythm of your poem. The third line of each stanza is inconsistent, which impacts on the flow of the poem.*
> * *Charles you are now at a stage in your writing where you need to be consciously crafting each line to maximize its effectiveness. If you are unsure, please ask for support.*

Charles responded to this feedback and produced a further revised version for publication in the school library:

Who am I?

I am a gluestick,

As stuck as can be,

I am a garage,

It's as tyrered as me.

I'm so sarcastic;

As you can tell.

The brightest of sparks,

A ringing bell.

I am a wizard,

A master with words,

I'm like a plane,

As high as the birds.

I am a tear drop,

The start of a cry,

A door always open,

So;

Who am I?

As we can see from this version, Charles has independently returned to his writing and has amended his poem to great effect. This example illustrates the whole reason for providing feedback. Charles has a good relationship with his teacher and values her expertise. He is then trusted to return to his writing and re-craft it for his own satisfaction and pride in preparation for display in the library. This is the work of a writer wishing to craft his work exquisitely, not merely the response of a child in pursuit of adult approval and judgement.

At Wroxham, we are keen to enable our children to become fluent writers and young authors. The children self-edit using a green pen from Year One upwards and in Years Five and Six they redraft using their own self-generated next steps for improvement gained from the modelling examples that the teacher presents and from specific feedback about their first draft. Teachers keep records of the development of skills such as spelling, grammar, punctuation and joined handwriting but the main focus is always on writing for meaning. On occasion, as a means of celebrating particularly hard-won progress in writing, we have printed and published children's writing in hardback book form for the school library. We learn more about one example of this at the end of this chapter.

Have we lost interest in what children have to say?

Too often, assessment of writing has become a reductive exercise that renders meaning as barely important. Armed with checklists of target skills, the voice of the young writer is drowned by a 'sandbagging' imperative to demonstrate grammatical devices and elaborate vocabulary. How can we regain balance and ensure that assessment acts as a means to inspire future development and authorial skill? Michael Armstrong, author of *Children Writing Stories* (2006), is concerned that assessment of writing has damaged English teaching. The next section, authored by Michael Armstrong, powerfully makes the case for another way of engaging with the assessment of writing.

The art of creative writing

We rarely give young children's creative writing the attention it deserves. It is as if we have lost interest in what children have to say. When we think of their writing we think almost exclusively of technique: of spelling and punctuation, vocabulary and grammar, formal address and stylistic convention. We read quickly and casually, pen in hand, eager to correct. In our concern for the predetermined standard we miss the value of the individual work.

How often do we provide space to gather together and study writing? The following story, written and drawn by a seven-year-old pupil in an elementary school in Boston, Massachusetts, was discussed at length with a group of teachers enrolled on an MA programme at the Bread Loaf School of English at Middlebury College, Vermont. It is important to emphasize the collective aspect of this interpretation. It is only in the joint close reading of a given text, with a variety of readers, that we are able to discount our own, individual literary prejudices. This is a very different process from teacher moderation aimed at justifying grades. Lack of time and pressure to judge can mean that we entirely lose the core purpose of children's writing.

The Gingerbread Place: a collaborative appraisal

What are we to make of this story? A close look at the roughly drawn title on the pink title page reveals traces of the word 'house' which the author has at some time erased in favour of 'Place'. We don't know why the author changed the title but the change is surely significant. 'Place' has a wider connotation than 'house'. It names not simply a building but the site of a plot. This is where the action takes place and, right below the title along the bottom edge of the page, we find the four figures that feature in that action, drawn in line, like actors in a forthcoming drama: girl, dog, stranger, house. The roof of the house is speckled with cherries

Figure 5.1 The Gingerbread Place

while a huge cherry, with a green stalk, tops the crown of the roof, as if announcing the house's name. The stranger and the dog look directly at the reader while the girl looks across to the house that she built. In the left hand lower corner, a speech bubble contains the author's name, Ceva Gabrielle Stanley. We may imagine her as the storyteller who has just finished telling her tale. This is her written version, which, now, we are about to read.

'Once there was a gingerbread house.' With these six words our young storyteller enters the imaginative world of the fairy tale. As it happens, the gingerbread house has little, directly, to do with the story. Its function is to place the story within the fairy tale tradition, with its familiar characteristics, a world in which it makes sense for a house to be built of gingerbread, a world that is ripe for magic. This is the place for storytelling, the traditional site that the author will appropriate for her own particular purpose. She is not copying or imitating; she is using tradition to fashion something of her own.

Ceva introduces her story with easy confidence. The five short sentences that make up this first page have a captivating rhythm. Each of them is rounded off with a heavily pencilled full stop. The second, third, and fourth sentences would conventionally be treated as a single sentence, containing two relative clauses. By treating the two relative clauses as separate sentences, Ceva achieves a special effect, obliging the reader to pause, before each clause, and attend to

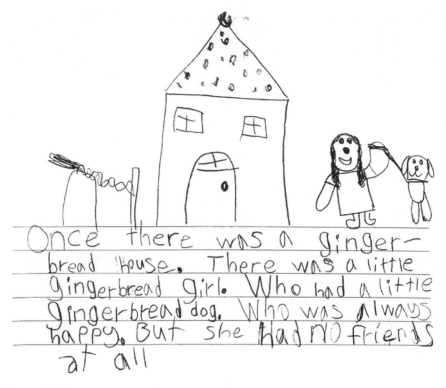

Once there was a ginger-
bread House. There was a little
gingerbread girl. Who had a little
gingerbread dog. Who was Always
happy. But she Had NO friends
at all

Figure 5.2 Development of Ceva's story

each item in turn: girl, dog, happiness. The effect of this particular punctuation becomes evident once the story is read aloud.

The fourth sentence is ambiguous. Is it the girl or her dog who 'was always happy'? The drawing suggests that it is both, the girl on her own account and the dog because, as we may intuit from the prominent lead, the dog is the girl's pet. But what about the words 'always happy'? The word 'always' is suspiciously unequivocal and suspicion is further aroused by the word 'but' which opens the final sentence and appears to cast doubt on the little girl's happiness. 'But she had no friends at all': how categorical the words 'at all' sound. They hardly appear to suit a girl who is 'always happy'. Can she be always happy but totally friendless? How about the dog? We wonder at the narrative predicament as we turn the page.

What is so striking about this first page is the way in which the author exploits the simplicity of her language. The most insignificant words 'always', 'but', 'at all', carry a wealth of implication, while punctuation lends the page a rhythmic clarity. Not a word is out of place. The predicament which the story will address is succinctly laid out for us, in words and images. Above the text beside the fairy tale house, conventionally drawn with its door, its inviting door knocker, its windows and its cherry filled roof, stands the little girl, holding her dog on a lead. Surely, we might suppose, the dog is the little girl's friend. It is not until the end of the story that we will understand why it can't be.

The second page celebrates the spectacular career of the heroine. There she stands, arms raised in acclamation, above the text. Building is her passion and she builds with the magical materials favoured in the long tradition of the fairy tale, 'cherries and gingerbread stuff'. She is supremely competent, 'she never messed up. Never!' the story insists, with an exclamation point for added emphasis. But the emphatic exclamation arouses once again the reader's anxiety. There is an ironic play between the words 'never' and 'always'. Their assumption of certainty only serves to harbour a doubt.

Anxiety is instantly justified. To turn the page is to be confronted once more by the word 'but', which is now separated from the rest of the sentence by a comma. The wary pause draws attention to the unexpected misadventure: 'one morning something was wrong'. Above the text, a speech bubble is filled with the single word 'Yikes!', shouted by the little girl as she lies in bed, wondering 'what had happened'. It is the only speech bubble in the entire story and it marks the decisive moment within the narrative, the moment that lays bare the limits of the little girl's self-confidence. The hole in her house represents, we might be tempted to say, the flaw in her character, or the truth she has still to learn. It is the unexpected incident, the misfortune, the curious event, which her overarching

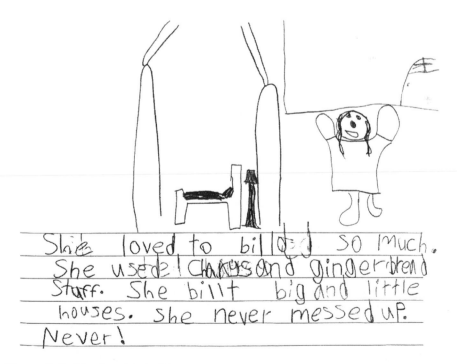

Figure 5.3 'She loved to build so much'

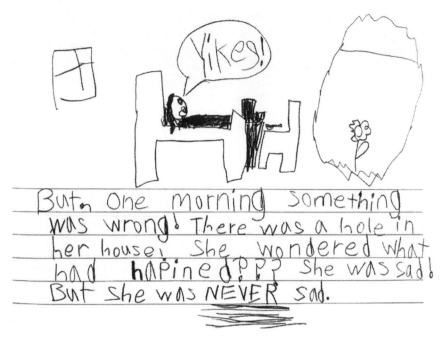

Figure 5.4 'One morning something was wrong'

confidence has in no way prepared her for. She sees that something is amiss and becomes suddenly sad. 'But she was <u>NEVER</u> sad', the page ends, recapitulating the end of the previous page. This time, however, the word 'never' is capitalized and underlined with a heavy scribble. By now we know that the word 'never' is never to be trusted. The wordplay is over.

Page four brings the story to a sudden halt. The little girl's mastery is no longer enough, the wall can't be mended: 'She tried to put it back on but it didn't work.' She bursts into irrepressible tears – 'Then she cried and cried and cried' – tears which, in the picture that accompanies the page, stream down the little girl's face, forming a blue pool at her feet. The tears are the mark of her incapacity; they blind her, the girl who 'never messed up'. Beyond the broken wall, a flower lowers its gaze in sympathetic alarm.

But the loss of sight is providential, for now the magic of the fairy tale intervenes to save her. 'Then something magic happened. Someone new came!' It seems to be the girl's blindness that gives magic its opportunity. The broken wall is replaced and sadness quickly gives way to excitement. We might have guessed that this supremely confident heroine would not be downcast for long. The drawing at the top of the page portrays with vivid originality the girl's excitement. How better to visualize excitement than to let the heroine jump right out of the page as the welcome stranger puts the broken wall back in place.

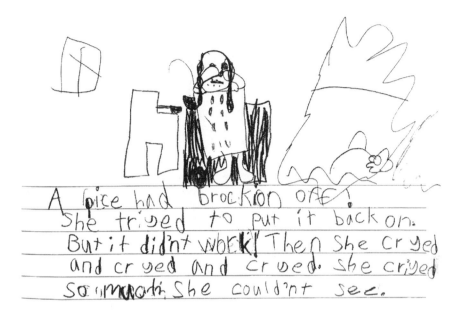

A pice had brockon off.
She tri
ed to put it back on.
But it did
nt work. Then she cryed
and cryed and cryed. She cryed
So
much she couldnt see.

Figure 5.5 'Then she cried and cried'

But who was this unexpected stranger? He hardly looks like the conventional fairy tale prince. The little girl needs to know. She asks him. His name turns out to be Mister Grass. The name is repeated no fewer than four times on this one page. It's not so much that the name is unusual, but that it is the act of naming that establishes a relationship between stranger and girl. It's the symbolic means by which stranger becomes friend. The girl will surely not forget Mister Grass, her new-found friend, and neither will the story's readers. In the picture above the text, a curious looking Mister Grass shakes hands with the little girl while behind him the broken wall has been nailed back in place.

So we arrive at the story's end. The girl, the dog and Mister Grass – curiously, the girl herself is never named – stand in line, the stranger and the child holding hands, the dog on its lead, as always. 'After that they were friends' the story concludes, but it adds a final thought: 'Finally she knew what it was like to have a friend.' So the outcome lies in the little girl's knowledge, rather than simply in her new friendship. Or, rather, the friendship she has found is what gives her the knowledge that she was missing. Happiness is not enough. Only friendship can make it complete. A friend is someone who can help, who can put things right, who can be a support in hard times, who can always be on hand. And now we see why her dog cannot be her friend, at least not in the same way as Mister Grass. The dog can be loyal and affectionate but it lacks independence. The lead, so prominently drawn in the illustration on page one of the story, is the ultimate sign of the distance between pet and friend. At the story's end it is still in place.

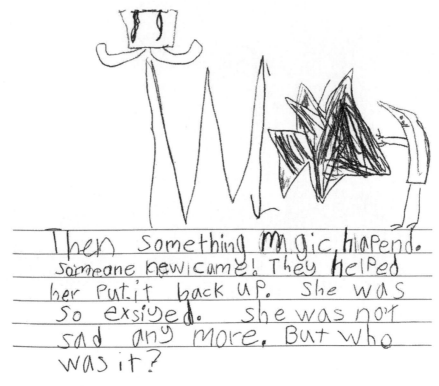

Then something magic hapend.
Someone new came! They helped
her put it back up. She was
So exsiyed. She was not
sad any more. But who
was it?

Figure 5.6 'Then something magic happened'

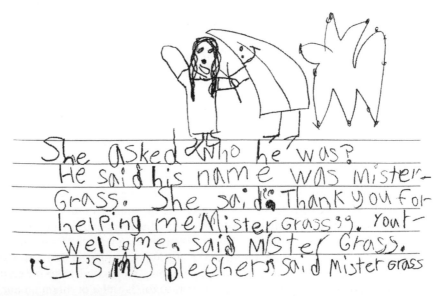

She asked who he was?
He said his name was Mister
Grass. She said "Thank you for
helping me Mister Grass". Your
welcome, said Mister Grass.
"It's my Bleeshers" said Mister grass

Figure 5.7 'Mister Grass'

After that, they were friends.
Fifinaley she new what it was
like to have a friend.

Figure 5.8 'After that they were friends'

The Gingerbread Place is a story that tells of many things: of knowledge, of friendship, of self-confidence and its limitations, of the unequal status of human beings and animals, of magic and the imagination. It tells us what its author has come to know in the act of writing her story. Paul Ricoeur, the great French philosopher of narrative, speaks of 'the power of fiction to re-describe reality', a quality of imagination that frees us to 'try out new ideas, new values, new ways of being in the world' (Ricoeur 2007: 174). This is very much how we might describe Ceva's achievement in writing *The Gingerbread Place*. She is using narrative as a way of exploring the human condition. In Ricoeur's terminology, she is applying 'the grid of an ordered fiction to the manifold of human action' (p.177). She is re-describing reality through story, rediscovering what Tolstoy, in his revolutionary essay on children's writing, called 'the beauty of expressing life in words' (Tolstoy 1982: 223).

In an enthusiastic, autobiographical aside, enclosed within a rectangular frame and added to the text as an appendix, Ceva acknowledges her delight in writing stories. 'Aother's note', she begins, in huge letters, 'I STARTED making books when I 6, in MS. BRENDA'S class. I useed to just make books. But then MS. BRENDA brot up a new kind of book making. I liked it so much, I did a lot of books. And I'm going to make more books.' That final sentence, characteristically introduced by the word 'and', which serves as an insistent after-thought, is both a promise and a prediction, and her handwriting grows still bolder as she declares her intention. It is an intention of the utmost importance, in so far as it signals the indispensable interrelationship between the making of meaning and

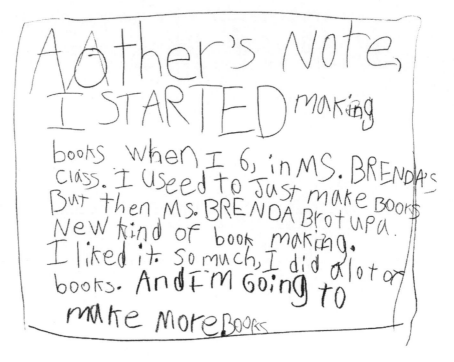

Figure 5.9 'Aother's note'

the exercise of skill, a relationship which contemporary discussion of education has all but set aside. Ceva's delight is what determines the skill with which she tells her story. It is evident in the zeal with which she manipulates punctuation to dramatize the ironic significance of words such as 'always' and 'never'. It is what focuses her attention on the dramatic significance of the comma, artfully placed after the opening 'but' on page three of the story. It evokes the rhythmic flow of the narrative, from the predicament established on the opening page, with its contrast between happiness and friendship, through the shock of the broken wall, and the little girl's scream, to the final moment, when the three protagonists, the little girl, her dog, and the newly befriended Mister Grass, can stand in line, facing the reader, taking their bow. In each case she finds the exact words, phrases and linguistic forms to convey the meaning she needs and satisfy her delight.

The tragedy of contemporary education is its refusal to have anything to say about children's delight in words. To read the programmes of study for writing in the national curriculum is a depressing experience. Children, we are told, must be taught 'to write clearly, accurately and coherently, adapting their language and style in and for a range of contexts, purposes, and audiences'. The emphasis is authoritarian and mechanistic. There is no space within this curriculum for spontaneity, curiosity, or open-endedness; no room for the play of language, no sense of language as living form. The outcome is predetermined; imagination is redundant.

But if there are no predetermined standards, then how are we to value the work of our students? The answer lies in the art of describing, the way in which we observe, perceive, and interpret children's works: their stories, poems, and meditations. Von Goethe (2006) put it neatly in the introduction to his *Theory of Colours*:

> For merely looking at an object is of no use to us. All looking leads to an observing, all observing to a reflecting, all reflecting to a connecting, and so we can say that with every glance we cast into the world we are already theorising.

The art of describing, in the setting of a school or a classroom, may be divided into four phases, or moments. First comes identification with the imagined world, the world of the 'as if'. We have to live imaginatively in the world of *The Ginger-bread Place*, with its wonderfully successful but self-satisfied heroine, the girl who never messed up. We have to share the shock of the broken wall, feel the heroine's violent mood swings from total despair to absolute exhilaration, welcome the magical arrival of Mister Grass, and absorb the story's ethical ending.

Secondly, we have to interpret the story through a detailed examination of its language, word for word. Interpretation, founded on close reading, lies at the heart of any attempt to understand children's work. Multiple meanings are not transparent, they are uncovered in the course of reading and re-reading the work, seeking to make sense of its ordered form. Of all the words in *The Ginger-bread Place*, the most significant is the word 'friends'. Friends is the final noun of the opening page and the final word of the last page. In between, we are given the narrative of a friendship, of the impossibility of life without friendship, of help freely given, of comradeship and mutual support. By the end of the story we too, like the heroine, have come to know, once again, what it is like to have a friend. We share her knowledge, informed by the beauty of her tale.

The third phase is that of critical appraisal and response. In *Children Writing Stories* (2006: 180), I noted that: 'this is the moment for questioning the author or authors, for sharing perceptions, exchanging interpretations, speculating together about the story's plot or its language, its characters and their circumstances, its twists and turns, its significance as a story'. It is also the moment at which we can examine the writer's skills, as demonstrated in her story, point to particular strengths and weaknesses, and consider how to address them. Part of a teacher's responsibility is to help students grow more self-conscious as writers and to appreciate the delicate balance between intention, intuition and chance in their work. But we should be aware of the ever present danger of imposing our own interpretation on the young writer. Appraisal is best seen as a collaborative, rather than an individual responsibility, involving all members of a teacher's class, writers, readers, and teachers.

The fourth phase looks to the future, to the books that the writer might read, the questions she might ask, the new styles she might adopt, the skills she needs to practise as she continues to play with words. Delight in words and word play is universal. It cannot be taught but it can be provoked, sustained, and enlarged with the critical support of teachers within a classroom that has been transformed into something like a writers' and readers' workshop. The tools the teacher might make use of to arouse and sustain delight are exceptionally various, from the reading of a master narrative of folk literature such as the story of Hansel and Gretel, to the provision of handmade booklets for children to write their own stories in. Nothing is too grand or too simple to arouse the children's imagination.

To interpret children's creative writing through deep observation and close reading is to give their work its due value. The aim is not to measure children's achievement against a predetermined standard, but to describe their literary works in a manner which recognizes their present literary concerns and promotes their literary futures, remembering that the goal is not to absorb tradition but to renew it. John Dewey, in his book *Art as Experience*, calls judgement 'an act of controlled inquiry' (1934: 304). If we think of assessment, in the teaching of creative writing, as controlled inquiry into the ways in which children make meaning, we can focus on how to help them sustain and advance their search for meaning as they grow. We have forgotten this for far too long.

(Professor Michael Armstrong, Breadloaf Teacher Network,
Middlebury College, Vermont, formerly headteacher of
Harwell Primary School, Oxfordshire)

Publishing young authors' work

Following on from Michael's contribution, our next example of the importance of taking children's writing seriously comes from Wroxham.

Nine-year-old Ashley Price, excited by a forthcoming visit from Anthony Browne, arrived in school with a package of manuscripts. He asked for an appointment with the Children's Laureate so that he could share his books about a certain 'Mr Wellington Boot'. At lunchtime, he nervously presented his work to Anthony Browne. The stories had been written at home, on the back of packing paper from the office where his mother worked. The humour, witty illustrations and sparing nature of Ashley's picture stories prompted critical acclaim from Anthony Browne. The discovery of Ashley's authorship coincided with a development project at Wroxham to transform a double-decker bus, bought on an online auction site, as a playground library and nurture space. Anthony Browne agreed to return to the school at the end of the summer term to officially open the library bus and also to attend a book signing of Ashley's published work. We arranged for Ashley's books to be typeset and professionally printed at a local firm. When the day of the bus opening arrived, the sun shone and Ashley proudly sat under a tree selling signed copies of *Amazing Adventures of Mr Wellington Boot*!

Figure 5.10 *Amazing Adventures of Mr Wellington Boot!*

(2010). Inside there were reviews from his class peers and on the back cover the following quote from Anthony Browne was proudly displayed: 'This brilliant book is a wonderful example of the amazing creativity that all children possess. The stories are richly imaginative and Ashley obviously has a huge talent – well done! (And keep writing!)'.

Early writing should be a form of playful literary exploration that extends beyond the confines of a classroom. Ashley's example shows us all why we need to be open to other ways of assessing the *adventure* of writing.

Summary

This chapter has reminded us of the purpose of teaching children to write. It began with consideration of ways in which teachers can use their own expertise as writers to help children explore how to develop their technical and aesthetic writing skills. Michael Armstrong then provided insight into the many layers of interpretation that may be given to a child's story when a group of skilled literary analysts take the time, collaboratively, to appreciate the meaning of a story. Finally, moving away from writing produced within the classroom with the teacher as prime audience, we heard about a series of stories and illustrations written at home using simple resources that nevertheless achieved national recognition.

The creativity that enables writing to become an art form provides a neat example of the professional dilemma presented by high-stakes testing. How far should we allow ourselves to teach with an eye to 'standards'? How can we regain equilibrium, recognizing that teaching writing skills in isolation achieves nothing if the unintended outcome is for children and young people to lose the art of writing? Enlightened assessment that refuses to label learners (or teachers), while fanning the flames of expertise, can be the means of achieving the balance we seek.

In the next chapter we hear of ways that schools are beginning to involve children in assessment dialogue with families. The examples we hear about go far beyond a bald statement of grades and move towards recognition of developing expertise across the full breadth of the curriculum.

6
Reporting to families: Sharing assessment without levels or grades

I like making rockets and testing them to see how far they can go. Also we blew marshmallows to see who was the best blower in the class. I came second. I want to get better at making boats.

(Alex, 7 years old)

The positive impact of engaging children and young people in the process of dialogue, learning and assessment is a central theme of this book. Within a culture of trust and openness, it follows that feedback to families should be an ongoing and informative process that continues the dialogue beyond school to home. In this chapter, we hear about the practice of schools that are moving beyond defining children in terms of numbers and attainment in English and mathematics towards a much richer and broader assessment of children's learning across the curriculum. We explore examples of schools that are increasingly confident about enabling children to become commentators and reviewers of their own learning. The work of Black and Wiliam (1998) provides evidence of the negative impact of grades as opposed to formative feedback. Providing detailed information for families is seen by the schools in this chapter as an opportunity not to issue a benchmark grade, but to engage in dialogue that celebrates what has been achieved, in order that much more can be learned.

From their earliest days in school, children flourish when they are given time and space to articulate their thinking and to engage in an ongoing process of self-assessment and review. This is most powerful, as we have seen, when it is not an abstract process but an active day-to-day reality, enacted through the opportunity to make independent decisions about learning, free of limiting factors such as labelling or 'ability' grouping. Individual feedback meetings and reports, presented in partnership with children, provide a means of engaging families in ongoing assessment dialogue that seeks to improve learning endlessly and throughout life.

Avoiding the label of 'hard to reach' parents

Brooker (2002), in her study of children starting school, found that the social and cultural capital of parents within the local community had an impact on children's capacity to thrive in school. Too often a perceived lack of engagement with the school by parents is judged as a failing on the part of the family, as opposed to recognizing that for many parents schools may be 'hard to reach' too. Leadership dispositions of generosity and empathy enable another way of communicating with parents. It follows that when we develop warm, positive relationships with children, this naturally extends to their families too.

Building on the principle that parents are the child's first teacher, schools in this chapter recognize the importance of establishing high quality, mutually respectful communication between home and school. At Wroxham, we realize that our children are powerful advocates for *Learning without Limits* as they experience daily in school the recognition of being valued as a unique individual. Families are warmly welcomed on the playground or in school at the beginning and end of the day with frequent opportunities to volunteer help within the classrooms or school grounds. Information about what goes on each day is provided via class blogs, email, Twitter and videos on the school website.

Family consultations

As mentioned in *Creating Learning without Limits*, Wroxham changed the traditional parents' evening to a more equitable format. When dialogue about learning is valued, it follows naturally that children should be part of learning conversations with their teachers and families. Instead of the school providing judgement and summative grade-related feedback to the parents, Wroxham holds meetings that include children. These meetings celebrate each child's strengths, while also highlighting areas where both school and home can support the child. As soon as possible, children are encouraged to attend family consultation meetings so that teachers can talk directly to them with their family present, instead of talking *about* them. Early Years teachers record short individual films using classroom tablets. The films are brief, informal and often include laughter; they are intended to provide a joyful glimpse of each child in school. Filming the children for an important meeting with their family provides an early formalization of the importance of building a language for learning. Watching their child and listening to their views offers insight to families about their child's experience of school and helps to illustrate their child's intellectual, social and emotional development.

This year, for the first time at Meredith Infants School in Portsmouth, teachers decided to involve the children much more in the summer reporting process. They decided to video every child presenting their report. Sharon Peckham, deputy headteacher, explains:

We wanted to enable children to speak freely about their learning experiences within the year, express their pride at overcoming challenges and explain their own steps towards mastering new skills and knowledge. We recorded each child using iPads and emailed every parent the video so that they could share their child's report with their extended family.

The school held a family consultation day where the parents, child and teacher sat together to watch the video, thereby providing an opportunity to jointly celebrate the child's achievements: *'The new way of reporting was fondly received by children, parents and their teachers. When teachers complemented each child during the recordings you could see children visibly grow with pride, one child in Early Years actually shuddered.'* The response from families was very positive, particularly as they were able to share the film with extended members of the family. One parent commented that *'it gave me a feeling of being a fly on the classroom wall'*, while another was pleased that the film provided 'a very nice way of showing progress'. One mum had become particularly anxious about her son. He would often cling to her in the morning before she left and the last thing she often saw was her child's unhappy face. What she didn't see was that he was invariably happily playing with his friends five minutes later and for the rest of the day. The teacher did her best to reassure mum but she continued to worry. During parents' evening she brought along her anxieties and concerns. Again, the teacher tried to reassure her he was doing well. When the video was played, mum sat back and watched a happy, confident little boy chat away enthusiastically about his achievements and next steps. Mum cried, it was the reassurance that she craved – she just needed to see it for herself.

This initiative will continue each year at Meredith with a video report added to the families' accounts every year.

Learning review meetings

Learning review meetings at Wroxham are held in the autumn and spring terms for all children in Years Five and Six. The meetings last for 15 minutes and are held in my office. Each child presents a set of slides illustrating their self-assessed views of their successes and challenges across the curriculum. The presentation is prepared independently by the child during lessons the previous week and serves as a structure for dialogue between the child, her teacher, her parents and the headteacher. During the meeting the child presents different areas of the curriculum in turn and discussion ensues about how to support her in learning the next steps to achieve further progress. The child or teacher may refer to work within her books to illustrate a point of discussion, thereby providing the parents with detailed insight into ways they may be able to support the child's learning. As headteacher, I attend all meetings across the final two years of each child's time in primary school. This means I gain insight into the child's self-review, the quality of her work, her relationship with her teachers and the support her family are able to offer. This provides a rigorous framework for formative assessment for all concerned. If the teacher suggests a course of action to support the child, we note this and ensure it is followed up immediately. Similarly, parents are aware that the meeting has high status and invariably they are keen to support their child once they are clear how this may be achieved. For example, if a child admits that they struggle to make time for homework we may all agree that coming into school early for 'toast and study' would be a good solution for all concerned. The essential message and importance of learning review meetings is that it is the child herself who is the most important participant.

Other schools have begun to adapt this format. At Bridgewater Primary School in Northampton, the children attend learning conferences with their parents and teachers to discuss learning linked to their termly report. At Banstead Infants in Surrey, all children from Years One and Two meet with their teachers individually during the autumn and spring terms to discuss their learning and to decide on next steps. In Chapter 4, we heard about their development of 'learning habits' that have enabled children to set their own targets (e.g. to be more *determined* when solving problems as a mathematician). Parents at Banstead report that the children are much more aware of their targets and refer to them at home. This was illustrated when Henry from Year Two was out for the day with his family at a National Trust property. He was taking part in a quiz and was required to choose an object to draw. A friendly guide offered to help him and advised him to pick an easy one. Henry replied that he was very *adventurous* and didn't need to pick an easy one. This was a child who had started Year Two saying that he did not need to improve on anything because he was already 'very good'. A developing understanding that learning is continuous enabled him to appreciate the importance of challenge and identify what he needed to do to improve.

At Greenfield Academy in Bristol, Kate Richardson decided to trial the first Year Five learning review meetings in June, in preparation for Year Six the following year. Earlier in the year, when she first arrived at the school, she had tried to ask children about their learning but they were unable to answer. By the summer term, having removed 'ability' groups, she was pleased to note a real difference in the capacity of the children to talk about 'how they learn best'. Visitors to the school also commented about the increased independence of the children during learning, their self-motivation to help themselves and their willingness to support others. Again, we note the impact of real-life genuine reasons to talk about learning when this is linked with developing independence and freedom from labels in the classroom.

Mark Carlyle, headteacher of Scole School, first trialled learning review meetings at the end of the autumn term with Year Six. The school team had spent considerable time working on a clear identity for their pedagogy, based on the fundamental principles of challenge and choice, resilience and independence; seeking to build pupils' self-awareness of their own learning. Mark decided to trial learning review meetings as he wanted a mechanism for the children to impart this knowledge to their parents and he was keen as headteacher to evaluate the impact of theory in practice. Year Six pupils created their PowerPoint presentations of 'successes and challenges' entirely independently. The children were encouraged to take the time to look through their books and think about their learning and the progress they had made. The headteacher made it very clear that he trusted them to decide what they wanted to share with their parents. One pleasing aspect of this, for Mark, was the degree of precision they achieved. They were able to pinpoint skills and dispositions for learning that they wanted to improve and they often prefaced these by using the phrase 'I want to challenge myself by . . .'

Mark recalls feeling 'surprised and impressed' by the way the children presented their PowerPoint presentation to their parents: *They all spoke confidently and articulately about their learning and there was genuine pride in their achievements.'* Mark was keen for the learning review meeting format to be primarily a conversation between the child and their parent, so although he scaffolded the process and occasionally prompted, he spent most of the time listening and encouraging. This provided him with the opportunity to jot down notes of any agreed actions and revealed to him how the children were capable of taking the lead and behaving as the expert. He was particularly impressed by the way the children demonstrated their knowledge of their learning by finding examples in their books to support the points they were making. On several occasions, he found that the children's confident self-reflections exceeded his preconceived views of what they might say. The supportive formality of the forum enabled the children to rise to the occasion and excel.

Time spent listening to children's presentations, reviewing their work alongside them and engaging in conversation with their teacher and parents is invaluable. The commitment to learning review meetings usually amounts to two full days and two evenings in the autumn and spring terms with some additional meetings for those families unable to attend on the dates initially offered. School leaders carrying out this role over time are able to build a rigorous picture of each individual child's strengths and learning needs while also supporting quality of teaching and professional learning in an enabling way.

Children's annual reports to families

In *Creating Learning without Limits* we refer to the fact that at Wroxham, instead of sending home a computer-generated attainment report for each child, we take time in the summer term to prepare a high-quality illustrated document in partnership with every child as a record of their learning throughout the year. This is an essential part of building co-agency, with teachers and children responding to each other's ideas and knowledge about assessment in partnership. The report format provides detailed feedback from both children and teachers about learning across the full breadth of the curriculum. Information about specific National Curriculum year group expectations is provided for families alongside termly summaries of future learning in each class.

The reports are written in the summer term using an agreed whole-school proforma. Children write an overall summary of their views about the year, followed by their self-evaluation of their learning in the core subjects of English, mathematics and science. The structure of the proforma means that each child has space to describe both their successes and challenges in each of the core subjects. The boxes are not fixed and some children may record several hundred words in each section, while others may record much less. The children's views about their learning across the foundation subjects are also recorded subject by subject with a response to each curriculum area given by their teacher. As the children move into the later years of the school, they work with specialist teachers for some areas of the curriculum. These teachers will be the ones that respond to each child's comment for their subject. A rich dialogue emerges as the teachers respond directly to the child's comment in the form of a written learning conversation. Typically, a report may run to four or five A4 pages and will include colour photographs chosen by the child. We teach the children how to proofread their work online and to use a spellcheck to ensure that they can be proud of their comments when they review them in later years. The reports are written by the children from Year One upwards when children are between 5 and 6 years old. Typically at this age the child will tell a member of the teaching team what they want to say in order that their views can be typed. Alternatively, older children can be tasked with 'buddying' with the younger ones to record their viewpoints. When this takes place, the teacher provides the older children with a curriculum summary for the year that they can use to prompt responses. Aziz, in Year Five, for example, may use the summary sheet to ask his Year One buddy to recall the class study of animals and Josh may show Aziz the map he drew when he was finding out about where animals were living in the school grounds: 'We *have chickens now because the eggs hatched in Year Five and now they are in a coop outside our classroom! I drew where animals might live in our pond and the woods and field*' (Josh, Year One report). This is then followed up with a response from the Year One teacher about Josh's engagement with the scientific study and his increasing knowledge about animals and their habitats. As the children become more proficient in their capacity to reflect on their learning, the reports provide an opportunity for each child to crystallize their thinking.

In the following report extracts, the quality of dialogue between teacher and child can be seen. Daniel, 9 years old, reflects on 'The Universe' topic that he studied during the past year with his teacher, Stephen Davy.

Year 4: 'The Universe'

> *I have enjoyed learning about a lot of things about the Universe including Nebulas, black holes, planets and orbiting. I really like the Universe as a topic because it's very interesting and things are happening right now.*

I found the stargazing evening quite fun because we got to go on an app called Stellarium where you can search through the solar system. We also got to make papier-mâché planets and we made holiday brochures for them. I really enjoyed writing the holiday brochures, because you got to make up your own planet and you could also add in things that they wouldn't have on Earth.

I enjoyed doing the Mars Curiosity Rovers because you had to make your own mechanical rover with things like sweepers and cutters. For the papier-mâché planets, I really enjoyed making them and painting them.

Stephen Davy responds: *Again, your reflections are outstanding and represent a rich learning experience. You should be very proud of this Daniel. Additionally, you should be incredibly proud of your progress through this topic and your impressive attempts to understand unimaginable sizes and concepts like planets and moons orbiting stars and then millions or billions of stars orbiting the centre of a galaxy. How many galaxies are in the universe? Do we know?*

A great achievement was your understanding of the basic building blocks of the universe, which are singular atoms/elements. When we learnt about this, you were able to use the periodic table to identify the atoms required to make water and carbon dioxide. This is an area of learning usually left to secondary schools, so you should be very proud of this.

I am glad you recall making the Mars Rover model in design and technology. Your design showed a great understanding of lever technology. Well done, Daniel!

Here is an extract from 10-year-old Lizzie's report with responses from her teacher, Nicky Easey.

English

Successes

One of my English successes is my spelling, I always check before doing the spelling tests. Also I always practise at home. My best success is my handwriting because when I was in year 4, I always did small writing and I did not do very neat writing because I always rushed. When I did 500 words I loved it because it was fun but it was also quite hard because I had written my story and there were only about 450 words. Then, I added more words so I had about 500! I am confident with my punctuation.

Challenges

I think I should add more adjectives and adverbs in my writing/stories. I find putting similes in my writing hard. Sometimes I forget that the rule in English is new speaker, new line. Sometimes I get about 1–10 words wrong.

Nicky Easey responds: *Your hard work at preparing for the spelling tests has really paid off Lizzie and you always do well in our assessments. This is a brilliant approach to take to learning and will take you a long way in life. Well done. You have developed your handwriting style this year and it is now a neat and consistent size. Brilliant. We have explored a range of fiction and non-fiction texts in Year Five and you seem to have enjoyed them all, learning about a range of features and developing your writing skills. You are varying the pace of your writing by using a range of sentence types; you could experiment further with this by including different types of dialogue (direct and reported speech). As you mentioned above, you just need to remember to start a new line for each new speaker. You have a good understanding of the structure of narrative stories and you are able to sustain ideas throughout your writing. Well done. I agree that you could include some more description in your work. This can be achieved by including some extended noun phrases (noun with verb, adverb and adjective) or by adding similes and metaphors. If you are not sure about these, please ask as we are happy to help you. Mrs Barker will also re-visit these techniques in Year Six. You did very well at writing your 500 words story and I know that you were very proud of your work. I also enjoyed reading your story about 'Polly the Giraffe' from your topic country.*

You are a prolific reader and this shows in your writing content. Well done. You have become more confident at sharing your ideas in our guided reading sessions. Discussion about the texts helps to build understanding and develop inference and deduction skills. You will continue to work on these in Year Six. I have also been pleased to see you being braver about reading your Newsround summaries to the class. Well done Lizzie, I know that this has been hard for you.

The quality of the interaction between the child and the teacher is vitally important to ensure that the report contributes to the child's developing understanding and the parents' opportunity to support detailed next learning steps. Simple comments like 'well done' may feel supportive but do not provide formative feedback for the learner to build on. The use of subject-specific vocabulary and technical terms from an early age gives the children the language they need to describe their learning. The headteacher reads every report and provides a brief comment. Written feedback from the parents is recorded and added to the overall document to provide a comprehensive ongoing annual review of each child's learning throughout the school. Report writing takes a lot of time but is highly valued by all concerned, as each document is highly individual and meaningful to each family. At Wroxham, a non-contact day to engage in report writing is allocated to each teacher, in addition to their weekly planning, preparation and assessment time.

The reports form a strong evidence base for progress achieved over time. Each year, before the summer break, a member of the senior leadership team cuts and pastes feedback from each child about their learning in mathematics and English to create subject-specific summaries from every cohort. These summary documents are passed on to the next class teacher and can be reviewed at a glance by the subject leader or phase leader. This part of the assessment process is crucial, as it ensures that the children's comments are acted upon in a continuous manner. Colleagues at Wroxham are keen to honour and act upon the feedback received year on year as each child matures in their learning. It is helpful and illuminating to see assessment as a continuous process as opposed to viewing the end of each year as a finishing point.

Formative feedback for children with additional needs

Anna is a vibrant member of our school community. She has Down's syndrome and is not always able to access the curriculum in the same way as the majority of her peers, however she is always included. The following extract from her Year One report illustrates the balance between helping Anna to join in with her peers and supporting her own unique development. As is the case for every Year One child, statutory reporting of the outcomes of the phonics check is embedded positively within the teacher's comments about English.

What I liked about Year One

I like playing with Jim and Chris.

I like going into the woods and making potions in forest school.

I like learning about vegetables.

The teacher responds: *It has been lovely watching you develop over the past year, Anna. You were able to settle into the Year One routine and your independence has increased. You came to school keen to take part in fun activities. You made steady progress in all areas of your work this year. You have taken part in PE lessons and have shown joy and perseverance when mastering gymnastics skills. I am glad that you have enjoyed Forest School. You were always eager to take part in the activities and you were happy to explore independently or with friends.*

You have a ready smile and enjoy having fun. You are an interesting and polite girl. It has been great teaching you this year and I wish you luck for Year Two.

English progress

I like reading and looking at books.

I liked the Enormous Turnip play and watching it on the blog.

I like Trevor.

The teacher responds: *Your English work and handwriting is becoming neater and you are continuing to develop your fine motor skills which are supporting your writing. Next steps for writing will be to continue to prac- tise writing your name and forming individual letters and writing a word/ caption alongside your pictures.*

Your reading has improved and you seem to get pleasure from reading but especially from listening to stories. You can read a lot of the Year One tricky words. I am glad that you like Trevor. Trevor Toucan has taught you all about the different ways of writing and reading sounds such as 'ee', 'ea' or 'e-e'. I am glad that you have enjoyed this, I will let him know.

You have not yet met the nationally required standard in developing phonics skills, but your progress this term has been good and continues to develop at a steady speed. Next steps for phonics will be to solidly learn all of the Phase 3 'sounds' and to consistently apply these in your reading.

I am glad you enjoyed taking part in the show. You did seem to have fun as a dancing turnip, you were very good. You joined in with the songs and actions and enjoyed listening to the various different versions of the story.

Pupil passports

St Mary's School in Barnet decided to develop pupil passport self-assessments with all the children. Inspired by the work of Swiss Cottage Special School, Lon- don (Lilly et al. 2014), Maria Constantinou, inclusion leader, was keen to develop pupil voice across her school:

This came at a time where, like us, the nation's schools were in transition in the movement to assessment without levels which naturally leads to a more personalized approach to target-setting. We chose therefore to attempt to combine the purpose of the document: to harness pupil voice in order to inform our teaching and provision and to focus the children's attention on the steps they needed to take to facilitate their progress further.

St Mary's developed a 'pupil passport' self-assessment report that is completed by all children. The one-page passport contains the following headings:

- things I find most difficult;
- things I like;
- additional support I receive and how often;
- what I have improved on;
- what I want to continue to improve on this year;
- things adults can do to help me achieve this;
- things I can do to achieve this;
- I will know I have achieved this because . . .

Whole-school developments such as this build on inclusive practice to ensure that every child's opinion about their learning is highly valued.

Breaking with the tradition of summative reports

When Kate Richardson became headteacher at Greenfield Academy in Bristol, she initially found that the children's poor behaviour was a huge issue and was impacting on learning. Within months she set about changing the culture through establishing an expectation that the curriculum should be irresistible and that all children's needs, interests and voice should 'be at the heart'. The school began to implement strategies for genuine pupil involvement and at the end of her first year Kate implemented report writing in partnership with the children. Kate was keen for the children to contribute handwritten comments in order that this would provide additional evidence of their learning development over time. However, this unintentionally caused additional pressure among some children who found it very hard to write without errors. When she asked colleagues to reflect upon the new report-writing process this was an area that some staff worried about, with one teacher commenting:

I think typing would be much better, as some children had to rewrite their reports a few times to get them right. It might also make parents take more interest in the content of their child's writing, not just the handwriting.

However, the overwhelming response from children, staff and parents was very positive. The reports were painstakingly produced and then presented by each child to their family at parents' evenings from Year One upwards. The meetings were up to 20 minutes long and many children enjoyed them so much that they commented the meeting should have been longer. Parents' responses included:

Loved it!

Great!

Really nice to hear what they [the children] thought.

Nice that they have a voice and some input – not just the teacher talking.

Easier to understand.

Really good – they enjoyed it and so did I.

I'm so proud of them – they are like little teachers.

I'm pleased they get a say in what to work on next year.

I'm pleased they know what they need to work on.

My child didn't like all the writing but it was worth it for something we can keep forever.

Teachers believed that because the children had self-generated their learning targets, they would be far more likely to remember them. They enjoyed the parents' evening much more and felt conversations had been very positive and focused on the children's learning. They also recognized that the children loved hearing positive feedback about them shared with their family. One or two children said that they disliked showing their work to their parents but they were very much in the minority. We have, very occasionally, experienced this at Wroxham and find it is usually related to underlying relationship difficulties within school or the family. Some of the Year Five children at Greenfield commented that they felt the new report format gave a 'more accurate' assessment of their work. They also felt that the process entailed *getting to know what we need to get better at'*. The Year Three children's comments included:

It tells my parents how I have done.

I knew what was in my report so it wasn't a surprise/shock.

Everyone was really proud of what I had done.

I liked picking my own work to show.

My parents were really proud.

We got to show what we wanted to learn about.

We got to say what we thought about our work.

It was the neatest handwriting I've ever done.

Children are keen to make the report into a booklet next year and to add pictures. They have suggested designing a front cover and including a self-portrait, the school logo and a drawing of their teacher within the document. Although the new report format took time to complete, the evaluative comments from all those concerned in the school demonstrate the impact that this kind of development can have.

Traditionally, Larkrise Primary in Oxfordshire produced reports for parents compiled using a web-based application with a bank of generic statements. This year, inspired by *Learning without Limits*, a different report format was designed. The new report includes photographs and pictures drawn by the children and consists of dialogue between children and teachers about:

- me and my learning;
- my maths;
- my literacy;
- what I have enjoyed and what I've learnt this year.

This is an extract from Dora's Year Four report.

Me and my learning

I love Larkrise because we do a range of different lessons. My favourite lessons are drama, science, literacy and maths. I also like music. In drama you can be whoever you want however in PE, science, maths, literacy and music you can learn lots of different things.

Miss Gold responds: *I think the fact that you have nearly chosen every lesson as your favourite sums up your wonderful, positive attitude to school and life! You have brought many laughs and lots of kindness to the Magpies Class this year so thank you very much!*

You always try your best in every single subject and have shown an incredible work ethic from day one. You certainly do enjoy a challenge, persevering at any task you are given whether you are working indepen-dently or in a group.

You have made amazing progress this year particularly in reading and maths. In maths I have really seen your confidence soar and I hope that you feel proud of your achievements in this area.

Commenting for a local newspaper feature about this 'new experiment', one family explained:

Child: *I really like these reports because we got to reflect on our own learn-ing and other people get to see what we think.*

Parent: *The biggest thing was that is really personal. I could hear my child talking about her learning. It brought a tear to my eye.*

Ed Finch, senior teacher at Larkrise, later tweeted: *'The parent response to our new style reports was huge, amazing, moving – such a force for good.'*

At Sunnyfields School in Barnet, teachers have found that children are very astute when it comes to assessing themselves and others. In their end of year reports, which they write and the teacher responds to directly, they can express where they have made progress and what they need to improve on. Through discussion with their teacher, each child agrees their next steps for the following year. Each child has reading, writing and maths targets that are used daily to support learning and to ensure that everyone is clear about the next steps. The targets are assessed jointly by the children and the adults. Children have become skilled at finding evidence in their work to justify their self-assessment. Annand, in Year Two, said, *'When I talk to an adult it helps me know the next things I have to do'* and Rex, also in Year Two, said, *'I can express my opinion about my work being done well, or what I need to work on.'*

Professional learning

Children as young as 4 write their own reflections and targets as part of their annual report at College Park Infants School, Portsmouth. Their headteacher, Debbie Anderson, explains that every child is expected to achieve', as the school motto of 'Children Playing, Improving and Smiling' suggests. She explains: *'It is far better to set the bar high for all and for everyone to achieve their own very highest results, than to set the bar low for everyone to just step over.'* Steven, 5, proudly writes, *'I am now a really good reader because I use expression.'* Five-year-old Alfie uses beautiful joined handwriting and his emerging phonic knowledge to write *'in my lerning I never giv up I chrigh my best'*. Felicity from Year One tells us: *'Writing is my favourite thing to do especially stories. I love writing stories because I add lots of expression. When I make a mistake I use a polishing pen.'*

In pursuit of excellence, Debbie's staff immerse themselves in a wide range of professional learning opportunities in order that they can deepen their own expertise and subject knowledge. An example of this was when the teachers attended art classes to improve their own skill at portraiture. Natalie, 7, was inspired to improve too: *'I have got better at drawing because last year I didn't do detail and I couldn't make them look that interesting. But now in year 2 I include both those things.'*

The shared belief that everyone is exceptional at something pervades College Park Infants School:

> *We offer a wide range of experiences and celebrate the many talents and skills of our pupils, hoping that we can enable children to discover a talent or interest that will change or influence the direction of their life: Phenomenal Philosophers, Great Gardeners, Super Scientists, Lovely Listeners and the list goes on.*

(Debbie Anderson, headteacher)

Figure 6.1 Natalie's portrait

Summary

In this chapter we have heard about actively involving learners in meetings with families in order that there is a shift of emphasis away from summative judgement towards an ambitious dialogue about next steps for improvement. Parents from the schools featured appreciate the depth of information that this process enables them to understand. Practical ways of supporting their child's learning are made much more obvious through the kinds of presentations that have been described. The need for constant grading and ranking diminishes if the message is clear that each child is able to illustrate the progress they are making and that they are keen to learn. In a culture without limits, children who are capable of exceptional achievement are free to excel.

Examples of end of year reports written in partnership between children and teachers have shown that this too can become a process that is dynamic and motivational. The specific detailed outcomes outlined in the National Curriculum (DfE 2013) also enable parents to see what is expected within each year group. The amount of detail that these meetings and reports share enables families to feel confident about the progress their child is making and provide a valuable supportive context to inspire the family about what has already been achieved, in order to help celebrate future success in partnership.

7

A whole-school approach
to assessment

We wanted to reclaim the language of assessment for ourselves.

Ela McSorley, Nishkam High School

This chapter examines how several schools, both primary and secondary, have developed a whole-school approach to assessment without National Curriculum levels of attainment. These are schools that have been brave enough to swim against the tide of continual tracking, focusing energy instead on ensuring that every child engages with high quality learning that does not predetermine what may be achieved. We explore the manner in which children's achievements are noted and recorded, rejecting the prevailing idea that learning is ladder-like, linear and predictable.

Monitoring progress at The Wroxham School

Tests here are not to see what group you are in. It is just a test really to see how you have done in the year and what you have improved on from last year.

(Philip, 10 years old)

Since becoming headteacher at The Wroxham School, I have undergone nine Ofsted inspections (three in the first year when the school was coming out of special measures). Every inspection between 2003 and 2015 required the leadership team to produce assessment data that provided evidence of past, current and future predicted attainment. While National Curriculum levels were used to report statutory assessment at the end of Year Two and Year Six, we utilized helpful assessment materials such as the Fischer Family Trust personalized data for our school and Hertfordshire software designed to track progress. However, the crucial difference between our school and many others was that we only used tracking as a failsafe background metric to ensure that every child's learning was noticed as opposed to using tracking to hold individual teachers to account or to report in-year or end of year grades to children and families.

At Wroxham we do not discuss grades or levels with children or families. However, we would not have achieved successive positive recognition from inspections over the past decade without a means of recording children's individual progress against the metric of National Curriculum levels and average point scores. We have used our whole-school assessment monitoring as a means to ensure that no child is overlooked and that faltering or exceptional progress can be identified quickly. While complying with a national expectation that data will be collected, we have nevertheless taken the opportunity to value this information as a springboard to generate questions that will support future *learning*, rather than as a means to provide *accountability* measures for teachers. Data are generated through shared discussion and review of children's work, self-assessment and test results, within a supportive culture of trust. Cross-moderation within our school and with other schools has ensured robust judgement. Many schools have become highly focused on relentlessly tracking individual progress as a means of providing evidence of effective teaching and leadership. Tracking, however, should be just that, a mechanism to provide an at-a-glance overview. A tracking overview of cohort 'performance' is only as useful as the questions and action that it generates.

What did we learn today?

How do we know what to teach tomorrow, if we do not know what the children have learnt today?

When the revised National Curriculum (DfE 2013) was published we met as a staff team to examine the detailed programmes of study for English, mathematics and science. Our first approach was to identify what had changed and to note the increased expectations, particularly within English and mathematics. Wroxham, in common with every other school in England, is keen to ensure that the curriculum provides all children with optimum success in statutory assessments. We therefore set out to balance increased expectations while maintaining a rich play-based Foundation Stage experience and high quality teaching across the full range of curriculum subjects. We are fully committed to providing children with the opportunity to excel in whichever areas of the curriculum they are most inspired by.

Our first step was to use the Assessment Framework 2014 developed by the National Association of Headteachers (NAHT) (see www.naht.org.uk). These key performance indicators grouped strands of the English and maths curriculum together, thereby reducing the number of areas for individual assessment. We used a simple format to record which children were confident in a particular strand of the curriculum following several lessons. We recognized that, in a highly inclusive school like ours, there would be some children either exceeding expectations or not yet meeting them. We developed a simple record-keeping grid that teachers could use each time they revisited a particular area of learning throughout the academic year, thereby noting the children's development over time (see Figure 7.1). At the end of the year, each child's attainment is recorded against the essential areas of learning on a cohort summary grid. The idea is not to aggregate scores giving each child a summary grade but to maintain granularity in order to understand areas of confidence and expertise and areas where further development, against the expectations of the National Curriculum for that year group, is needed. The summary grid is coloured in green and white. We deliberately did not use red boxes, unlike many tracking systems that use a 'traffic-light' approach, as

---

Year 3 Unit Evaluation

Date: March

Subject: **Mathematics**

Key Performance Indicator: *Can recognize, find & write fractions of a discrete set of objects: unit fractions & non-unit fractions with small denominators*

Learning objective(s):

Name	0	1 **Emerging** At early stage of development (support needed)	2 **Securing** Growing ability and independence (prompting needed)	3 **Secure** Exhibits skill independently	4 **Mastery** Exhibits skill spontaneously and with confidence
Alfie			2	3	
Ben				3	4
Chi			2	3	
Dravit		1	2		
Finn	0	1			
John				3 3	
Nida			2	3	

Other comments:

Finn has an education support plan updated to illustrate progress

Figure 7.1 Record-keeping grid

the colour red implies 'stop' which is distinctly unhelpful. The purpose of the grid is to act as an assessment summary for transition between year groups. We do not share the numbers allocated against attainment with either children or families as these are merely indicators against current learning. There is no aggregated score as this could only be used for ranking purposes. We are interested to note which specific areas the child is not yet confident in, so that we can ensure we build on all areas of learning as the child proceeds through the school.

When Ofsted conducted a pilot maths subject inspection of Wroxham in June 2015, we were readily able to convince the visiting inspector of the robust, informative nature of our assessment system. He talked to children, studied their books, observed how children engaged with learning during lessons and triangulated this with the summary cohort grid. He also looked at assessment files and lesson study notes. At no point did he attempt to convert our data into equivalent National Curriculum levels, point scores, or similar. His expertise thereby enabled him to report on the high quality of mathematical learning across the school.

Inclusive assessment practice

As a highly inclusive school we are very keen to support every child's learning and to celebrate every step of success. Where children are not yet able to meet the demands of the National Curriculum year group expectations, we ensure that we keep a richly illustrative portfolio of learning evidence in partnership with the child. Much of this learning may be stored online through video clips and photographs, but we also keep detailed records of individualized planning alongside the child's books. This allows everyone, especially the child, to recognize and document success.

Early intervention

In order to ensure that we have strong institutional memory about each child, we keep a confidential summary document that relates to any child where we have a concern about home circumstances, learning needs or emotional needs. This register is kept up to date by our inclusion leader and ensures that we have an ongoing record of every aspect of support that we have provided. This record also includes information such as whether a child is eligible for pupil premium funding or speaks English as an additional language. Alongside this summary document, we also analyse individual behaviour records that contain details of any incidents that occur in school. These individual records are summarized electronically and enable us to note any patterns of incidents.

Learning journals

As much of the learning in Year One is practical and not always recorded through writing, we also use photos and observations for much of our assessment.

Examples of this can be seen on the class blog and in children's folders. We are also in the process of developing electronic journals which will document key moments throughout each child's learning throughout school. This will be used to record evidence of speaking and listening, observations of practical learning, and pieces of work that the children are particularly proud of. We aim to build an electronic record of each child's learning, which the children will be able to add to and access independently, allowing them to share their achievements at home and at school.

Written formative feedback

Our approach to written feedback is to ensure that the focus is always on supporting learning. We are aware of the current practice in many schools to insist on so-called 'dialogic marking' in books as a means of providing evidence for external accountability purposes. As we saw in Chapter 5, where the teacher and child engage in feedback and review that builds expertise and agency in the child there is a place for detailed marking. However, we are clear that feedback is for the children and should be useful. Books do not always need to be marked for learning to have taken place.

An example of co-agency is the current development within our Year Five class of a system of checking work through the offer of worked examples that children can use to self-assess and mark, using green pen. The advantage of this is that children are able to see where they may have become confused and can work with a learning partner to resolve issues mid-lesson. They are also trialling a system of symbols in the margin for specific types of feedback that mean their teacher avoids writing the same comments in lots of books. It is useful for each teacher to copy several examples across a year, that illustrate how a child's thinking has been extended following feedback (whether spoken or written) about a specific piece of work. This serves to underpin the core purpose of formative assessment which is to enable the child's understanding to grow.

Quality of teaching

In *Creating Learning without Limits* we describe the benefits of a harmonious learning collective where adults and children work together to discover 'natural balance' through a culture of trust and co-agency. Within such an environment, there is no place for ranking teachers. In partnership with governors, teachers lead inquiry such as lesson study, where a particular focus or particular child is studied, in order that together new ways of building learning capacity can be uncovered. Performance management at Wroxham has never been tied to percentages or point scores of progress but continues to be based on a holistic review of the children's experience of learning throughout the year. Successive judgements by Ofsted over the past 12 years have confirmed outstanding teaching and standards of achievement throughout the school. Evidence of successful teaching is easy to gather within a school where children and teachers know their learning is valued. This form of leadership for learning leads to high expectations through peer review and is much more enabling than a culture of fear based on assumptions of uncovering deficit.

Progress meetings

Together with our inclusion leader, Cheryl Mence, I attend progress meetings with each of our class teachers every term. We set aside time to talk about each child. In preparation for the meeting, teachers update their assessment files and in some cases copy examples of the children's writing for shared study. I prepare a class record sheet for our meeting that includes details such as date of birth, home language, pupil premium status and any additional needs, with a large space for written comments. Progress meetings have become standard practice in many schools but at Wroxham this is not a discussion about tracking or future test scores. Instead, a pedagogical conversation about each child's learning takes place. As a headteacher, my role is to ensure the highest quality learning experience for every child and the best possible teaching experience for every adult. As we settle down to discuss each child in Year One, for example, we may talk about the transition from Upper Foundation, friendships, growing independence, children's capacity to listen and engage in dialogue. Essentially, I am keen to ensure that every child is emotionally secure and able to learn. We look at each child's developing writing skill and discuss the books they are reading and we hear about the curriculum and the children's responses.

There may be times in the conversation when we stop and puzzle over a particular child. In our most recent Year One meeting, the teacher, Emma, commented: *'Hmmm, I'm quite worried about Greta . . .'* This followed on with a description of the things that Greta was finding difficult to learn. Listening carefully first, we then discussed together how we could all find a way through to help Greta to overcome some of her challenges in learning. We talked about how we could provide additional practical resources, how we could develop strategies to help her explain her thinking, how we could observe her play and her independent learning during a lesson. In short, instead of Emma using the child's additional needs as an excuse, she was enthused and supported in a discussion about how we could all discover more about Greta, in order to help her. We went on to have similar conversations about other children, some of whom were reading and writing fluently already. How could we make sure we were maintaining each child's interest through offering more challenge? What about Jonny, whose father regularly visits the classroom after school to ask for updates? How could we reassure him further? What kind of problem-solving activities could we offer Elise, who already knows her multiplication tables? How could we support Lin to voice his opinions?

Trust is the underlying factor that enables each meeting to become a sharing of pedagogical expertise. If I had seen my job as one of holding each teacher to account for their performance, the conversation would have started and finished with a data sheet. Tracking is not assessment, progress is not linear and teaching is not easy. Instead of a focus on tracking, which we simply use as a background metric, we engage in a professional conversation to build knowledge about how to inspire future learning. This alternative experience of a 'progress meeting' offers so much more, as it provides a genuine, open opportunity to develop insight and expert knowledge about each child.

Developing subject knowledge

Whenever we begin teaching a new area of learning at Wroxham, we are keen to know what the children's existing knowledge and misconceptions are. Anne Goldsworthy (Naylor et al. 2004) has worked with our teachers to develop their expertise in teaching science. We have adopted her advice about finding simple ways of asking children to self-assess their prior knowledge at the beginning of a unit of work and demonstrating their enhanced understanding at the end. One activity she describes is to ask children to draw labelled diagrams that they can then revisit and adapt after several weeks of study. This simple activity enables teachers and children to clearly see what has been learned in a specific area such as digestion. Progress can be summed up, by asking children to record:

I used to think this . . . and now I think that . . . because . . .

I used to think this . . . and I still think this . . . because . . .

Other activities may include explaining what has been learned via presentations (see Chapter 3) or through group activities such as putting salient facts into song lyrics. At the end of last term, Nicky Easey, deputy headteacher at Wroxham, gave the children an alphabetical sheet entitled 'What I know about Extreme Earth . . .' as a prior learning assessment that the children will enjoy revisiting as their geography topic develops through the new term. The point is to engage the learners in the process of self-review and make new learning visible as described by Hattie (2012). It is also worth noting here that teachers' own subject knowledge is vital when planning lessons that are open-ended. Similarly, when providing formative feedback for learners, teachers need to understand the conceptual progression within that particular subject. The expertise offered by Subject Associations provide inspiration, support and advice in this area.

Assessment of reading

We assess reading in a wide variety of ways. From the earliest days we are keen for children to be excited about reading. We work closely with parents and children, encouraging them to change their books as frequently as they wish, without a limit on the number of books they can take home. We quickly find that children who may be encouraged to race through banded reading material at home will ultimately only happily read with their family if the text is accessible. This approach enables families to feel confident that their child is not being 'held back' if their book is not changed by the teacher on any particular day. The issue for us is not how many books go home but how we can encourage every child to develop a love of reading and to become discerning about choosing books that are not too easy, or too hard. We have invested in our library and have employed a part-time librarian to support children in choosing books for independent reading.

We regularly assess the children's reading and phonics, and keep a record of their progression through the different book bands and phonics phases, which enables us to immediately move on any children who are ready for the next challenge. We keep individual reading records and records from guided reading. In older classes we have established reading circles, where classic literature is read as a group. This enables all children to participate, even if the text under discussion is not one that every group member would be able to access independently. We encourage reading for performance and encourage reading for pleasure through provision of high quality reading spaces, including access to the reading bus on our playground every day.

Children who find learning to read challenging are supported through more regular practice and focused support using programmes designed by the teachers. The emphasis is always on including every child and exposing every child to high quality literature. Our core aim is to ensure that all children are reading fluently and with enjoyment as soon as they are ready to do so. At present, our approach is to focus detailed assessment of reading only where children are finding early literacy skills unusually difficult. Where this is the case, we analyse which aspects of reading the child needs additional support with and provide this accordingly. Our expectation is that every single child will become a fluent reader.

Expert learners

Stephanie Storrar, the headteacher of Banstead Infant School in Surrey, a three-form entry infant school, explains how her school developed the notion of 'expert learners' among their 3- to 7-year-old children. The school values each child as an individual and has never used the language of National Curriculum levels, or grades, with children or parents. The leadership team at the school use educational research as a means to lead school improvement. The work of Shirley Clarke (2014), Guy Claxton and Bill Lucas (2015), Carol Dweck (2012), Jo Boaler (2010) and the ideas of *Learning without Limits* (Hart et al. 2004) helped the school move forward and to make learning a shared process of co-agency.

Banstead has used formative assessment as a method of self-evaluation for many years. Through discussion and modelling, the children generate learning objectives and devise success criteria. They have become adept at using these to evaluate and identify their next steps in learning. In the Early Years and Year One this was initially teacher led but the children very quickly became experts and improved upon the success criteria devised by the teachers. As a result, the teaching team recognized that teacher-devised success criteria needed to be more child-centred. Learning objectives improved as teachers thought about the learning from the children's perspective, which in turn led to clarity and improved teaching. Alongside success criteria, the children also use 'learning habits' as a way of self-evaluating their work (see Chapter 4).

When National Curriculum levels were removed, the school initially turned to a look-alike software system but headteacher Stephanie commented: *'I was not happy with what we did last year which was basically replacing levels with pseudo-levels. We were using software which broke down the bands into b, b+, w, w+, s, s+* [beginning, working within, secure].'

Fuelled with confidence by the recommendations of the Commission on Assessment without Levels (DfE 2015), Banstead has begun recording children's progress throughout the year using a termly 'windscreen' format, as shown in Figure 7.2.

Using National Curriculum criteria, along with formative assessment and individual meetings with the children, teachers record current achievement on the windscreen. The example represents the first assessments of the academic year, so the majority of the children are 'emerging' within their year group band. Some have achieved a number of the 'expected' objectives and so are shown in the expected section. As the year progresses, teachers would expect the children to move from left to right across the windscreen. For those children who might not reach the band for their year group, the school has developed detailed individual windscreens for the band they are working in, so that everyone can value and record their progress.

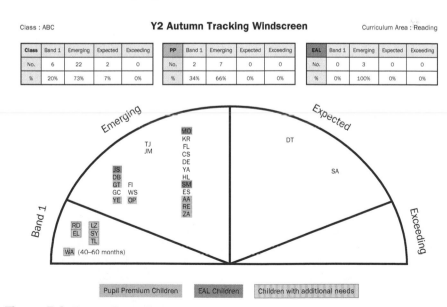

Class : ABC **Y2 Autumn Tracking Windscreen** Curriculum Area : Reading

Class	Band 1	Emerging	Expected	Exceeding
No.	6	22	2	0
%	20%	73%	7%	0%

PP	Band 1	Emerging	Expected	Exceeding
No.	2	7	0	0
%	34%	66%	0%	0%

EAL	Band 1	Emerging	Expected	Exceeding
No.	0	3	0	0
%	0%	100%	0%	0%

Figure 7.2 The tracking windscreen

A simple spreadsheet is used to track the children's progress from their different starting points, ensuring that factors such as date of birth, English as an additional language, pupil premium status and additional needs are clearly recorded. In the Foundation Stage, assessment is mainly through observation of the children and through dialogue. Elsewhere, progress in the children's books is reviewed alongside termly meetings with teaching teams. Alongside formal arrangements such as these, ongoing professional dialogue is part of a daily process.

Developing an assessment app

Other schools, such as the innovative East Barnet Secondary School, have taken the opportunity to design their own progression system to enable students, parents and teachers to understand details of what they are aiming to achieve in each subject. Recognizing that progression looks different across subject disciplines, East Barnet School departments are each developing ways of enabling their students to recognize steps of progress towards excellence. Keen to engage students in self-assessment, the school is developing an app to support this process. The English department has conceptualized the core areas for assessment within an English 'brain' (see Figure 7.3).

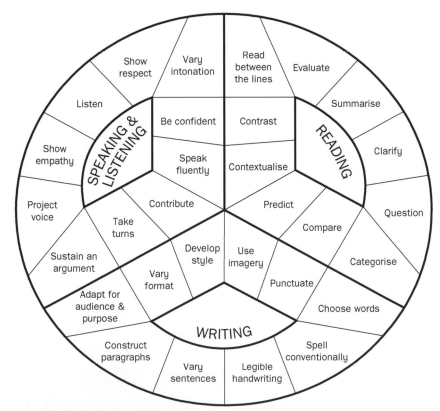

Figure 7.3 The English 'brain' (East Barnet School)

Taking ownership of assessment and devising means of making progression accessible to all students is one of the most promising aspects of the current movement beyond national curriculum levels in England.

Linking assessment to curriculum design

Ela McSorley is assistant headteacher of the Nishkam High School, part of the national cross-phase Nishkam Trust. As a new school in the third year of operation, in a deprived ward of inner-city Birmingham, Nishkam High School is ambitious for its students, who are aspirational and have chosen to attend because of the values and dispositions upheld by the school. Ela reflects:

> We were excited and driven by the government's announcements about the end of National Curriculum levels. We had debated formative and summative assessment, trialled different ways of giving feedback, but not yet broken free entirely from the 'known quantities' of National Curriculum levels. We knew what we wanted to do: help our children to succeed academically and to become good human beings, loving learning, enjoying school, with a zest for improving the world around them. Feedback in the form of levels and sub-levels alone wasn't going to do that. We needed and wanted something which measured students' progress and which spoke to them directly about what they needed to do to improve.

Nishkam is committed to developing an exciting and unique all-through education rooted in faith, values and 'sewa' (the Sikh term meaning to serve others). The national changes to in-school reporting of attainment and progress provided an opportunity to create an assessment model across the trust. This needed to be a system that accurately captured the progression and learning of all students through the Nishkam curriculum from Early Years through to Key Stage 5 and beyond:

> We imagined a system without compartmentalization . . . a system which mediated against transition gaps and a lack of continuity and consistency – a system which is connected to the curriculum and developed in a way to support learners' learning and progression, co-constructed by teachers and learners, parents and governors, across the trust. We believed this would be better for our young learners and, in addition, better for our teachers who would gain the chance to see the learning journey in its entirety and be able to plan a curriculum with assessments that are meaningful, useful and fit for purpose, recognizing the importance of the assessment and planning cycle. We didn't want categorization of progress by levels and numbers.

The process of arriving at the new assessment system involved all stakeholders and took time. Firstly, they discussed what they *didn't* want from an assessment system; namely categorization of progress by levels and numbers. They wanted their system to describe and articulate the learning and progress their students made; and they wanted to reclaim the language of assessment for themselves. They also wanted assessment reporting to be helpful for parents and learners and easy for everyone to understand. Moreover, they wanted to ensure they were not placing a ceiling on achievement by setting targets that seemed to be self-fulfilling. They were clear that progress is not always linear or uniform and they sought a way of recognizing and valuing this.

Reclaiming assessment

Colleagues at Nishkam spent time arriving at a set of principles to help guide them in their work, which they could return to at difficult moments or to help with decision-making.

Principles

- All students can and will achieve.
- Intelligence is not fixed; attainment is not predetermined.
- There should be no ceiling on achievement.
- Students do not fail, they just have not succeeded YET.
- Assessment as well as targets (and education) should enable, not limit.
- Everyone can strive for subject mastery, and should be encouraged to achieve this.
- Assessment is to support learning and the learner to make progress.
- Marking and feedback is for students and should clearly and articulately describe what the student has achieved and what they need to do to improve.
- Having passionate advocates for each subject who can exemplify and provide examples of mastery and success is motivating for *all*.

Alongside these important principles, the trust agreed the following.

Five statements of assessment practice

1 One of the biggest impacts on student performance is teacher feedback.
2 Teachers must know their subject, syllabus, exam, as well as their learners and the context in which they are operating, alongside what learning happens immediately before and after their phase of teaching, in order to accurately assess and have a positive impact on students.

3 Numerical/grade/level targets often have a detrimental impact on students' motivation and should be used with caution.

4 Teachers need to know and recognize excellence in their subject, as well as progression, in order to provide opportunities to grow and nurture excellence in their subject.

5 Teachers need both their subject knowledge and their pedagogy skills in order to assess and provide feedback in a way which is constructive, helpful, supportive and motivational.

A rich demanding curriculum worth assessing

Colleagues at the school were faced with a number of key questions as they embarked on their work. They researched many other schools and systems, in the UK and across the world. They were concerned to create a 'simple and easy to understand' system for all stakeholders that could be applied consistently across the curriculum. They were also keen to discover ways of tracking short-term progress, describing 'excellence' and building even higher expectations for all learners. As they worked through these issues they began to realize that this was not just about assessment, but was also about the curriculum. In order to assess learning and progress the teachers needed to ensure that the curriculum was fit for purpose, engaging and exciting, and mapped out to ensure progression. The aim was to provide ample opportunities for students to strive for excellence.

Notions of subject mastery

The team at Nishkam debated subject 'mastery' and decided that while students could aspire to and strive for subject mastery, mastery is almost always out of reach. Ela McSorley explains the debate:

> Working towards mastery is something that motivates and drives the committed student to constantly improve upon previous best, but can that be attained while the student is still in the early phases of learning? We believe in our high school (and indeed in the other phases) excellence is achievable, although still beyond most students' grasp, an A* at A level or GCSE or the new Grade 9 are recognized marks of excellence. We stuck with the word excellence. But we had to be sure that teachers knew what this looked like and knew how to create opportunities for students to work at this high level.

Subject departments working in partnership with primary colleagues were tasked with the following questions:

• What do students need to master in terms of knowledge, understanding and skills in order to be successful at Key Stage 4 and beyond?

- How does Key Stage 3 link to Key Stages 4 and 5? How does one phase support smooth transition to the next? What about life beyond Key Stage 5?
- What does excellence look like in each strand of your subject?
- What does progression towards excellence look like?

Do we know what excellence looks like?

The first step that Ela and her team took in articulating 'excellence' was to identify what this would look like in each strand of every subject, thereby determining the end goal while the student continued to study that subject in school. Recognition that learning is a lifelong process was also agreed. Having agreed a definition of excellence the teaching teams were able to work backwards from this to determine the steps, increments in skills, knowledge and understanding to support students to get there. Teachers begin working with the National Curriculum, analysing the purpose, aims and content for each subject into accessible 'can do' statements. Mapping these, alongside their newly developed descriptors for excellence, enabled teachers, students and parents to see progression in each strand of the subject. The example in Figure 7.4 is from the history department:

Name	Date		Teacher		Assessment
Historical skill	I can	I can	I can	I can	I can
Analysing sources and evidence	Read different types of sources	Extract facts from a source	Explain what a source is trying to tell me by establishing the reason why it was produced	Evaluate the reliability of a source by looking at who wrote it and their motives for writing it	Assess how useful a source is to historians investigating a particular event or period in time
Essay writing and debating	Include facts within my work	Describe what happened during a certain situation	Explain my point of view	Produce a balanced argument and give my own opinion as a conclusion	Include interpretations of historians to add weight to my argument

Figure 7.4 Nishkam High School history KS3 assessment feedback (*Continued*)

Chronol-ogy	Order events on a timeline	Identify where events fit in within a certain time period	Identify change and continuity across different time periods	Analyse why there is change and continuity across all different time periods	Analyse the extent, speed and impact of change and continuity within a specific time period
Causes and consequences	List the causes or consequences of an event	Describe the causes or consequences of an event	Explain the causes or consequences of an event	Link the causes or consequences of an event together and explain how they are linked	Prioritize the causes or consequences of an event and be able to distinguish between short term and long term effects

Figure 7.4 (Continued)

Ela reflects:

Some subjects were more straightforward than others; the linear nature of maths lent itself to this type of work, whilst subjects such as English were much more complicated in the sense that excellence demands the application of skills, knowledge and understanding across a range of genre and form also (notwithstanding the split into language and literature by KS4 and KS5). However, our teachers relished the challenge and colleagues engaged in some exceptionally useful professional development as nuances in language were debated as they revisited the curriculum, realizing that some aspects of the school curriculum were not allowing for students to demonstrate excellence or that some experiments/projects/trips were no longer fit for purpose. Colleagues also 'climbed inside' their own subjects, so that they really did understand progression and excellence within their field.

Thinking cross-phase

The team at Nishkam High School knew it was important to work across phases. Many meetings took place with senior colleagues across the trust discussing how to track progress, how to ensure their system would be robust enough and support the learning and development of every child. In addition to this, professional learning events were held for colleagues to share work carried out across the trust, so that transition from one phase to another could be made as seamless as possible. Developing understanding of progression in this way provided crucial professional development, especially for subject specialists engaged in curriculum development.

Consulting the students

It was also important to consult with the Nishkam students. Almost all of the students spoke about the importance of teacher feedback. While some baulked at the notion of the removal of National Curriculum levels ('How will I know I have done the best I can?'; 'Getting a high level motivates me') all agreed that comments written, verbal or both, helped them to improve. What was clear was that students wanted to know what excellence looked like, in order to strive for it. They also wanted to be challenged, in an environment that was supportive and nurturing:

> *Our feeling was that levels sometimes got in the way of this, either because teachers felt under pressure to demonstrate sub-levels of progress rather than spending time on aspects of the curriculum needed by the students in the group, or because too many students found an absence of challenge, limited by levelled work, that didn't allow them to think and develop skills in a broader way.*

Changing mindsets about assessment

Having engaged in a full-scale review of assessment practice across the trust it became apparent to the teachers that National Curriculum levels and sub-levels had often become a measure of school (or teacher) efficacy sometimes quite removed from what they were supposed to be doing: measuring a student's progress and attainment. In all of this work, it was important to change the mindset (of teachers, parents and students) so that everyone agreed that this was about helping students to improve and that *all* students can improve.

Many of the teachers had been concerned about measuring progress in the absence of levels. Collectively, and in departments, considerable time was spent talking about the importance of using the language of the subject in order to articulate achievement and progress. A student can make progress in history, for example, if she learns to question the validity of the source she is using, rather than simply responding to what she sees or hears. The concept of validity enables the student to move to a more sophisticated comparison of source material in her writing. This articulation of subject progress is altogether more useful and meaningful than the teacher-speak of 'he has moved from a 4a to a 5c'.

Unfortunately this shorthand had become common currency and was used as the means to compare school performance.

Information for families

Early work with parents was crucial to the prospect of the new assessment system being accepted, understood and valued as an improved opportunity for educational discourse. Colleagues at Nishkam knew that it was important that all stakeholders became advocates for a system that eschewed levels in favour of a closer focus on learning and progress. Materials were developed for parents, including a handout and a presentation to be used during parent information meetings. Plenty of time was allocated for questions and to reassure parents, who were predominantly worried about a potential slip in standards if numerical targets were not being set. In response to this concern, teachers emphasized their expectation that all students would strive for excellence. Teachers illustrated the way that they had mapped out the curriculum to relentlessly encourage and enable opportunities for students to work at a high standard. It was emphasized that this was not a reduction in rigour but a means to support teachers to focus on teaching their subject, providing feedback that would ensure all students knew what they needed to do to improve:

> *The response from parents and students has been very positive, as we have embedded into our new system the language of our own values and dispositions. None of this is an add-on or a system we have borrowed, we have looked again at our curriculum and decided the most appropriate ways of assessing learning and progress.*

The commitment to collective problem-solving, research and engagement with professional learning is evident. The development work that has been undertaken at Nishkam High School is an example of what can be achieved when colleagues work together in an environment of trust, where principles and values inform practice.

Summary

This chapter has presented a range of whole-school approaches to recording and tracking learning and progression. The schools featured have all taken the opportunity presented by national assessment reform to introduce systems that they believe will not only provide the management information needed but will also reduce any tendency towards labelling of learners.

In the final chapter, we bring together all the issues discussed throughout the book to consider the transformative impact that a pedagogy of hope can have on school improvement.

8

Principled innovative leadership for transformability

> *We were recently inspected, during SATs week for a second time, and were thrilled as a junior school to come out of 'requires improvement' and be rated as* good *across all areas. We are continuing to embed a culture whereby children have choice of challenge. I personally feel that using this approach has transformed my teaching.*
>
> (Kath Burns, St Nicolas CE Junior School)

In this chapter we consider the impact of principled, courageous leadership. Insights from other school leadership teams, which have transformed learning communities through building professional expertise, empowerment and trust, illustrate what can be achieved. Eaton Primary School in Norfolk, for instance, improved swiftly after changing direction and abandoning 'ability'-based practice. We hear about the successful inclusive vision of Bridgewater and Rosendale Schools. The secrets of the sustained 'outstanding' achievement of the highly regarded Morpeth Secondary School London are shared by their longstanding leadership team. The chapter ends with an update about our work at Wroxham and the development of the Wroxham Transformative Learning Alliance, committed to inclusive professional learning. Finally, consideration is given to the potential impact that could be achieved if schools put into practice the kinds of pedagogical, curricular and assessment approaches described throughout this book.

Moving from 'inadequate' to 'good' in less than a year

In November 2013, Eaton Primary School, Norfolk, received the devastating news that Ofsted judged it to be 'inadequate'. The headteacher left the school and a new leadership team began work. Although they were committed to moving the school forward, morale was very low and the team found it difficult to know where to begin. They started to research articles and publications about effective learning and leadership. Time was allocated for staff discussions about classroom organization, grouping and the curriculum. The teachers' viewpoints were mixed. Many teachers had never stopped to consider the impact of differentiation or learned helplessness. This meant that children were placed within fixed groups and were not encouraged to challenge themselves. Most of the time only those children judged by the teachers to be of 'higher ability' were offered an extension task. Lucy Coy and others on the leadership team began to understand the reason for Ofsted's view that the school had unacceptably low expectations. It became clear that some classroom practices were unintentionally limiting children's opportunities to learn and might be holding children back. This was the complete opposite of what they wanted to achieve as teachers.

An alternative to ability grouping

The discovery of *Creating Learning without Limits* (Swann et al. 2012) was a turning point for Lucy and her team. The 'challenge approach' practised at Wroxham was very different to any others that teachers at Eaton Primary had come across. They were struck by the insight that in many schools the practice of 'differentiation' unintentionally often equated to limiting and labelling children:

> *The opportunity to be liberated from ability grouping was daring and radical, but also felt exciting. We were interested to try this for ourselves. We knew that we had to act quickly to improve the school. Inspectors were visiting and reporting on a termly basis and we had to record any aspect of proposed improvement within detailed action plans. We began by holding meetings with teachers and teaching assistants to present and discuss the 'Learning without Limits' ideas alongside those of John Hattie [2012] and Carol Dweck [2012].*

(Lucy Coy, deputy headteacher)

Taking on board many of the ideas from *Creating Learning without Limits*, senior leaders actively engaged the whole school community in their improvement journey. They implemented the classroom pedagogy, discussed earlier in Chapter 5, that has become known as 'choice and challenge', thereby eradicating so-called ability grouping, in favour of giving children the opportunity to self-evaluate their learning. After 18 months of working in this way, the children at Eaton were surveyed about their learning. The response was overwhelmingly positive. They loved the freedom, independence and responsibility conferred on them through the notion of challenging themselves. Here are some of the children's comments that particularly stand out:

I like the challenges because when you do hard things you learn new things.

(Billy, Year One)

Yes. I like the challenge approach. I don't know what I would do without it!

(James, Year Two)

I feel good when I am learning because I am being listened to.

(Ellie, Year Three)

I extremely enjoy the challenge approach because I used to feel trapped inside and I wouldn't have any confidence but now I do!

(Joe, Year Four)

The challenge approach is good because it gives me the choice to do harder work.

(Aimee, Year Four)

I am listened to because when I say something, people don't judge it they accept it.

(Tom, Year Five)

I know the teachers listen to me because almost all of the time they take in our ideas and use them.

(Jack, Year Six)

I like the challenge approach because it expands my mind.

(Robert, Year Six)

Listening to children

Lucy wrote an action plan inspired by the principles that staff had taken from *Creating Learning without Limits*. One of the key areas of the action plan was to include the opinions of the children. Colleagues realized that the children's voice should be considered as equally important to that of the staff. The action plan was designed to be as simple as possible so that it would be easy to implement across the school. Working with the entire teaching staff, a whole-school resource pack was designed with six circle-time sessions for the teachers to use. Circle-time meetings began to take place weekly in class with teachers and teaching assistants leading discussions with the children. In order to have the greatest impact on the school, it was agreed that every class would stop their morning activities for circle time every Tuesday at 11.45 a.m. All staff joined in to listen to the children and share ideas. The circle-times focused on a number of questions for the teachers and children to explore. The topics included discussions about how to overcome challenges and how to develop a growth mindset. Each circle time taught the children how to be independent learners and how to challenge themselves. The children were also taught the vocabulary needed to describe their learning.

Introducing the 'challenge approach'

As well as the circle times, whole-school assemblies also focused on the challenge approach and were led by the interim headteacher. Storybooks were purchased with similar themes to the weekly circle times to help further embed the challenge approach on a whole-school level. By this point, all of the staff were fully involved: *'The challenge approach has helped to accelerate the progress that our children make. It has enabled teachers to engage children in conversations about their learning. It has helped us to raise expectations and to enhance our curriculum'* (interim headteacher).

At the same time, teachers slowly began to implement 'challenges' in their classrooms in place of attainment-based grouping. They took away the fixed 'ability' labels and started extending the children's freedom to learn by offering all of the children the chance to choose their own level of difficulty for English and mathematics. Staff began to allow the children to sit where they wanted, depending on the resources they needed and the level of challenge they were attempting.

Help stations were set up in the classrooms with resources from which the children could help themselves. Discussions with local cluster schools inspired teachers to develop 'challenge scales' (see Figure 8.1) which were then displayed in all of the classrooms. Children were invited to comment on how challenging they found their learning on a scale from 1 to 10. Children were taught very carefully about how to become independent learners and how to know which challenge was right for them. The children were also taught how to move up or down

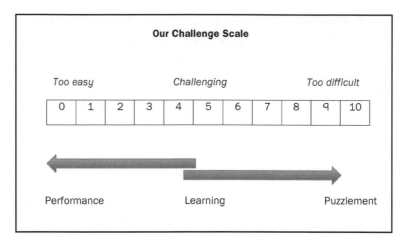

Figure 8.1 Challenge scale

the level of challenge if the task was too easy or too hard. They were encouraged to change challenges without the need to always wait for their teachers' approval: 'As a newly qualified teacher who struggled to set effective differentiated tasks throughout my training, I have found that the challenge approach has revolutionized my approach to this essential area of teaching' (newly qualified teacher).

A parent information session was held to explain the ideas behind the new approach to learning. At first, some parents were sceptical, believing that children would opt for the 'easier' challenge in order to complete the task more quickly. The initial findings showed the opposite – children were tackling work above the level where they might have previously been expected to do so. This was illustrated to parents via pupil interviews that were filmed and shown at the meeting.

Impact on staff

The teachers and teaching assistants were given time during weekly professional development meetings to discuss the circle-time sessions and how well the children were adapting to self-differentiation. Gradually, colleagues realized that the ethos behind the challenge approach – having the confidence to try something new, evaluating good learning and not limiting their aspiration – was starting to have a profound effect on the staff themselves. Lucy noted:

> The staff began to gain in confidence. Morale began to improve; the challenge approach had opened up a new sense of trust within the staff. Teachers became more confident about sharing ideas and talking about their understanding of how children learn. They began to listen to each other's ideas about how to embed the challenge approach. They also talked more

about what the children were saying in their classrooms. Gradually, the children's feelings and opinions were becoming a bigger part of the conversations during staff meetings.

Children were also encouraged to spend time talking and listening to each other. They were taught how to respect each other's individual learning needs and that nobody's learning capacity was fixed at any given time. Expectations were raised as all of the children were given the opportunity to stretch themselves, and their progress began to improve: *'Ever since we started doing the challenges it has boosted my confidence and knowledge because it gives you more freedom, rather than being trapped in a challenge that is too easy or too hard'* (Ellie, 8 years old).

Whole-school improvement

There was a clear impact on attainment, with a higher proportion of children achieving beyond the expected level in SATs tests at ages 7 and 11. Writing results improved significantly and staff began to see other improvements in many areas of learning across the curriculum. The children were excited by their new approach to learning, and this had a direct impact on their learning behaviour: *'Because we have challenges, we can choose our own work so we don't get bored. We don't mess around in class because the lessons are more fun and more interesting'* (Joe, 9 years old).

Lesson observations confirmed that the children were challenged more in their lessons than before and that there were fewer incidents of passive or negative behaviour. Lisa, one of the Year One teachers, was inspired:

Since adopting the challenge approach the children are more conscious of their own progress. They can clearly see how they have improved, as they begin to complete challenges that they had previously found difficult. The children are willing to experiment and try challenges that are more complex. The regular circle-time sessions have helped prepare and inspire the children to take on new challenges, by creating an ethos based around perseverance and a 'have a go' culture.

Initially we were sceptical about allowing the children to choose their own level of challenge; now that we have implemented the technique, it is clear to see how the challenge approach has motivated all our children. The children want to be proud of themselves and they enjoy a sense of achievement when they complete a new challenge. This makes them less likely to choose a challenge below their current understanding, or if they do, they quickly reassess and decide to switch to a challenge that is more rewarding.

(Lisa, senior teacher)

Parents were excited by the new approach to learning as well:

I'm convinced that this is a way of working that benefits all types of children and learning styles from the quiet and cautious to the most able and ambitious. I have been impressed with the way in which the 'challenge' concept has been embraced right across the school. It seems already to be a core part of the school's fabric for teachers and pupils alike.

(Parent and member of the interim executive board)

As a school in difficulty, change needed to happen quickly but required a strategy that would allow both rapid and *sustainable* improvement. Ultimately, Eaton School moved from a category of 'special measures' to 'good' in just under one year: *'The new "challenge" curriculum is successful. It has made school more enjoyable and productive for pupils, who now develop the skills they need to learn quickly and securely'* (see www.eaton.norfolk.sch.uk).

Lucy Coy has become a passionate advocate for pedagogy that refuses to set limits:

The challenge approach produced instant results across the school. Children were inspired to challenge themselves and become better learners. Teachers were reinvigorated and began taking risks with their lessons once again. The test would be if this initial launch would fizzle out. Not so – ten months later and we went from 'special measures' to 'good'. Months later, and progress continues to improve throughout the school. We have begun a journey of discovery about how children learn and how to encourage the children to challenge themselves and to become independent learners. This experience has completely changed the view of the staff. We now realize that children's abilities are not fixed and that children should always be offered a range of challenges to choose from. Teaching teams have learned to allow the children to have the freedom to learn at their own level of difficulty. Eaton Primary School is now a school that embraces inclusive learning and firmly believes that all children have the capacity to learn and to challenge themselves. Intelligence should not be limited or fixed, but instead it should be encouraged to grow and develop. It is our duty (and our pleasure) to see our children enjoy their learning. After all, watching children learn, explore and discover are the most exciting things about teaching.

The improvement story at Eaton is fuelled by optimism and the energy that comes from change that, although difficult, feels emancipatory. The next school that we visit offers a further example of leadership that has been similarly brave enough to 'swim against the tide' and adopt an approach inspired by professional learning.

Rejecting ability grouping and labels at Bridgewater School

Bridgewater is a rapidly expanding primary school that has rejected notions of fixed intelligence in favour of a liberated pedagogy of listening to children. Alison Harvey, headteacher at Bridgewater, recalls a groundbreaking moment in 2011 when the Early Years leader returned from a conference and announced that she was no longer going to teach phonics in groups but would keep all the children together in classes so that every child could access the learning. Alison vividly recalls this moment:

> *I took a deep breath and said, 'Ok then let's give it a try.' It felt a bit risky, but we could monitor the situation and adjust accordingly. In a very short space of time we could see the benefits before our eyes. All children were empowered and as a consequence there was writing hanging up everywhere in Early Years. Boys were literally running to get pencils to write up their lists in the garage in the outdoor area. It tied in with our creative, thematic curriculum where 'real' situations provided the vehicle to encourage writing. We were off!*

Alison recalls that colleagues throughout the school started talking about the positive impact of removing ability grouping in the Early Years and soon Key Stage 1 began to build on this. The influence of Dweck's theory of growth mindset (Dweck 2012) gathered momentum too and further resonated with the inclusive ethos of the school. This thinking was characterized through seven 'learning heroes' including Captain Co-operation and Dr Don't Give Up: *'The children were soon talking about resilience and perseverance and that to make a mistake was a good thing as we had to make a mistake to learn something new. The language of challenge and high expectations was everywhere.'* The pedagogy and curriculum offered at Bridgewater help to create a culture of opportunity that encourages hard work and an intrinsic motivation to challenge yourself. Roberto, in Year Five, recently relayed the following description in an assembly when the discussion was about it being healthy to learn from mistakes. Alison recalls:

> *If you get a page of greens (correct answers) you are going around in a circle, and he demonstrated this with his arm. He then said, 'But if you get a pink (an incorrect answer) your learning is expanding and moving forwards in a spiral,' which he also demonstrated.*

The culture at this school is one of 'no child slipping through the net', which comes about through quality learning and teaching and 'solid' formative assessment leading to differentiation through challenge. Alison Harvey is convinced about the profound impact that removing ability groups has had:

> *Our staff say it would be hard to teach ability groups of children now. How could they stand in the way of any child reaching for a challenge and having*

the confidence to work resiliently to develop deep and ultimately a profound understanding of their learning? We can't imagine now the extreme scenario of being labelled as a low achiever in Early Years, stuck in bottom group and kept there throughout their schooling with no aspiration! Why would you bother making an effort when no one gives you a chance to thrive?

The next school story we feature is Morpeth School, a London secondary school that has achieved sustained excellence through a relentless collective ambition for every student. This is a school in a tough urban environment that thrives due to a highly inclusive culture of trust and co-agency. Morpeth serves to remind us of what can be achieved over time when core principles enable and sustain excellence.

Placing trust in teachers

Morpeth School, Tower Hamlets, London, has been consistently recognized as an outstanding secondary school over many years. Alasdair Macdonald, headteacher until 2013, worked closely for several years with Jemima Reilly and Laura Worsley who now lead the school together as headteacher and associate headteacher. During their most recent Ofsted inspection in 2013, one of the inspectors asked the leadership team, 'Why is morale so high in this school?' Alasdair, headteacher during the inspection, reflects:

We were of course pleased to hear this but equally shocked as well. Why should an inspector be so surprised to find that morale is high? Why, when so many people join the profession with moral purpose, determined to develop their professional skills and make a difference to our society, should morale be so low in so many schools? Have we reached a situation where high attainment and high morale are incompatible? We believe not, and more importantly, we believe that high staff morale based on professional development and trust is essential if we want genuinely outstanding, innovative and creative schools.

All schools have a unique culture at their core. This leadership team believes that schools need institutional consistency with core values permeating all relationships and learning. Jemima Reilly, headteacher, explains:

We want our pupils to be successful, inquisitive, independent learners and we feel they can only be this if their teachers are encouraged to be this as well. Everything that we do is underpinned by these two principles – that pupils want to learn and attain highly and that teachers want to grow as professionals and develop their teaching. It is then the role of leaders, by consistently modelling behaviour based on these beliefs, to enable both staff and pupils to take up their roles.

Building a school with this ethos has taken time. The leadership of Morpeth has had considerable continuity in terms of personnel but, even more importantly, in terms of values. Twenty years ago, Morpeth was struggling with low attainment, very challenging behaviour, a loss of confidence in the school and low morale. None of the other changes would have been possible without first addressing the structures and systems of the school and thereby creating a safe and secure learning environment. Good behaviour for learning is necessary to support and liberate both staff and pupils. The leadership team knew that they had to create order for real progress and learning to take place. However, they also knew that they had to show, in all their actions, the values of trust and positive relationships that they wanted to be at the heart of the school. Schools, especially those in challenging circumstances, are fragile. Leaders need a fundamental belief in what they are doing and this must be evident to all in their daily practice. Alasdair, Jemima and Laura reflected:

> We would be dishonest if we said that we knew all of this when we started. Much of it was not articulated and some of it had not even entered our consciousness. We, the relatively new leadership team, knew that we had to deal with all the challenging aspects of a struggling school, while at the same time retaining our values and recognizing that the way with which we dealt with pupils and staff and the relationships we established would become models for the whole school. But we were also very aware of this being 'work in progress' and that we were continually learning and developing our vision and our understanding of the school.

As we have seen throughout this book, successful learning communities raise achievement and attainment while, at the same time, creating an exciting, challenging and innovative environment for staff and children. It is important to include Morpeth's story in order that we can celebrate evidence that it is never too late for children and teachers if their school improves.

Together, the team has identified significant stages of the school's development, underpinned by values and consistency. Each of the phases interconnects and overlaps, closely resembling those discussed in Chapter 1.

Creating positive learning behaviour

The first stage of the school's improvement focused on behaviour for learning. At the outset, attendance was well below 90 per cent; there was a significant issue with truancy from lessons; behaviour in many classes was very poor and a small minority of the pupils prevented the majority from learning. In the corridors, playgrounds and on the streets around the school, the authority of the teachers was continually challenged and much of this poor behaviour was related to racial tension. There was some good teaching and one or two departments achieved good exam results, however there was far too much poor practice. One key factor was common to these issues – the school did not have the capacity to follow up consistently the multitude of issues that arose every day. The pupils knew this and knew that poor learning and behaviour would probably not be followed up at all, certainly not consistently. The leadership team took the decision that, however time-consuming it was for them, the pupils needed to see that there were always consequences from their actions. It was crucial that strong relationships were built and that staff were actively supported. Almost immediately, leaders were confronted by a microcosm of the issue they would continually encounter. Should they go for the quick fix, the top-down 'we know what is best' approach?

'Listening to the pupils was essential in building trust'

There were huge levels of mistrust between the different ethnic groups and frequent violent incidents. Rather than deal with this solely as an issue of behaviour, an 'away day' was organized for a mixed group of Year Eleven boys. The team recall: *'The morning session was disastrous with attitudes verging on hatred being expressed, and at lunchtime we thought we had made a huge mistake. However, something happened over the informality of lunch and in the afternoon real progress was made.'* The wider implication for the leadership team was that the importance of *listening* to the pupils was essential in building trust. The telling-off, the brief call home and the punishment might all be necessary, but these actions would not change behaviour. In the classrooms, when dealing with challenging behaviour, leaders did not want to create a situation where the 'strong' staff would be able to manage but the majority would continually struggle and have to pass on issues to senior staff. An insistence on strict, almost military-style discipline would not empower either the staff or, more importantly, the pupils, who needed to learn to take responsibility for their own learning and behaviour. Expectations had to be clearly stated and insisted upon, but not through force, or a retreat to 'You will do it because I told you to do it'.

Staff begin to actively support each other

In order to change this element of the school's culture, senior leaders, heads of year and tutors all had to 'buy in', but the lead came from the headteacher and deputies modelling the approach that they wanted. Slowly, behaviour, attendance and attitudes to learning improved and, crucially, the nature of relationships started to change. All staff, not just those with charisma and powerful personalities, and irrespective of age or experience, could, with this approach, create the right conditions for learning in their classroom. A fundamental shift took place as staff began to actively support each other, collectively taking responsibility for pupil behaviour. In *Creating Learning without Limits* (Swann et al. 2012) we describe this as a 'collective endeavour'.

Staff became increasingly involved in all aspects of the school's development and started to take on a large measure of accountability for their own work and outcomes as they identified with the school's emerging values. The vast majority clearly felt liberated by the trust invested in them and new staff were attracted by the progress being made but, in particular, the school was noticed for a strong emphasis on professional development. The leadership team found they were increasingly able to appoint staff with a diverse range of ideas and backgrounds but crucially with similar core values. When mentoring sessions and discussions took place with new staff and student teachers, they almost unfailingly commented not only on how they felt incredibly well supported by colleagues but also on the trust invested in them.

'*Our leadership was based on a positive default*'

Although there was definitely less pressure than is currently demanded by Ofsted for a 'quick turnaround', the team knew that in the second phase of development low levels of attainment needed to be addressed urgently:

> *All our principles and ideals would soon founder if we were not successful on the standard measures being used by government and Ofsted. Could we raise attainment without reverting to a leadership style that controlled every detail of what teachers did, and trusted nothing that hadn't been checked?*

Again, it would have been easy for the leadership team to adopt a 'top-down' approach. Looking back, they are in no doubt that at times they had to use 'shortcuts' but they were equally determined to take staff with them. Placing trust in staff, as the key means to achieve school progress, was vindicated over and over again:

> *At every stage the staff demanded more of themselves than we ever would have asked, gave more of their time in what might be called discretionary effort and equally held themselves to account at least as rigorously as we or Ofsted would have done. Of course there were some staff that did not 'buy in', but they were in a small minority and it was crucial that our leadership was based on a positive default – that our staff were professionals who could be trusted.*

Throughout this book, the transformative impact of trust has been explored and, at Morpeth, this principle is not a 'soft' option but one that avoids viewing teachers and children in a deficit manner. The outcome was that increasingly the leadership team experienced staff goodwill, pupil commitment and parental support. Results improved, morale in the school rose rapidly, Morpeth became a popular and oversubscribed school and attracted excellent staff.

Building cultural and social capital

The leadership team became increasingly aware that higher attainment on its own was not enough. Education is about more than exam results. The school was committed to a 'broad and balanced' curriculum, including experiences beyond the classroom, and this became the cornerstone of Morpeth's third stage of development. This resonated with staff who wanted breadth and depth of experiences for the pupils and who gave willingly of their time. Alasdair Macdonald is concerned, however:

> At present, in England, we are in danger of creating a new 'gap' in our education system. We may succeed in narrowing the attainment gap, only to find that pupils from disadvantaged backgrounds face another, huge barrier: a lack of cultural and social capital, compared with more middle-class children, arising in part from the impact of a very narrow exam-focused curriculum. In particular this gap may be apparent when comparisons are made with those attending independent schools where the pupils receive an education that embraces not only a broad and balanced curriculum experience, but also diverse opportunities in sport, the arts and personal development.

Support for learning, aspirations and enrichment

The staff desperately wanted education to be more than just GCSE or A-level results. Hence they were more than willing to run business mentoring programmes, lead educational visits and residential trips, organize theatre and other cultural visits and also, importantly, recognize the value of such experiences and, where possible, release pupils to participate. The institutional consistency spoken of earlier came into play, as those three elements applied to staff as well. The school leadership team worked hard to find ways to support staff who wanted to study and develop their skills and knowledge; recognizing and supporting staff aspirations both personal and professional, while also ensuring that opportunities for enrichment were supported or provided for all staff.

Developing pedagogical skill and repertoire

The developmental stages of Morpeth's journey often overlapped and coincided. Throughout the school's development there had been a focus on teaching and learning. However, the most recent focus has been on improving pedagogical skill and repertoire still further. Building on the trust and relationships developed over time, the leadership team placed increasing emphasis on pedagogy, on professional development and on shared leadership of teaching and learning. This is symptomatic of a new professionalism based on the empowerment and leadership of good and great teachers, within a self-improving system. The culture at Morpeth embodies one of professional learning. Inspired by the environment in which they are working, reflective practitioners constantly seek ways to improve their practice and thereby the attainment of their pupils. In consequence, morale is indeed high and illustrates what can be achieved when school improvement is inspired by belief in the development of teachers.

Outstanding achievement without 'ability' grouping

At Rosendale Primary School in London, headteacher Kate Atkins wanted to resist teaching that labels children by 'ability'. To try to achieve this they made three significant changes:

1 Ability groups were abandoned.
2 Independent learning became a key part of every day.
3 Children develop metacognition through self-assessment.

Kate acknowledges that it has been a challenging journey but one that has seen improved outcomes for children both academically and socially. The initial challenge was how to support teachers to change long-established practices, while ensuring consistency in a large three-form entry primary school. Without a doubt, any change necessitates time and persistence. Sustainable and fundamental changes in pedagogy do not happen overnight and require a supportive yet rigorous programme to oversee that change. Professional learning and co-agency needs to be enabling, inspired and continuous, as we found when researching *Creating Learning without Limits*.

When considering how to move away from ability groups, it became clear that what Rosendale needed was a pedagogy that offered clear guidelines and processes for teachers to follow, as well as one that provided high quality training and materials for staff. Over the last four years many whole-school training days have been devoted to the theory and practice of this pedagogy. A consultant works with the school, coaching staff on their practice and setting the next series of action points for staff development.

This has been a significant investment for the school in both time and money, but one that has led to improvement in the quality of learning in classrooms. Classrooms at Rosendale have been transformed. Children work in mixed teams of four that change every half term, meaning that they work with every other child in the class, which increases their social circle and teaches them that everyone has something useful to contribute. This philosophy of teaching is one that promotes cooperation and ensures that no one can 'opt out' of learning. Whole-class teaching has become much more dynamic with increased opportunities for children to rehearse learning and support each other. Independent work is no longer differentiated, with children left to struggle on their own. Children work as coaches for each other, deepening their own learning while also utilizing Vygotsky's 'zone of proximal development' (1962). Children, and importantly adults, see themselves as capable of accessing all learning. There is no glass ceiling.

This new approach also changed how the school day is structured. Each day begins with children completing self-selected independent activities. These are often activities that will reinforce previous learning. There are also high-level challenges available that *all* children can access. The children select which activity they will complete each day and the staff discuss with them their choices and how those choices are supporting their learning. This initiative proved challenging for both staff and parents and entailed plenty of discussion, development and explaining to get right. However, the effect it has had on the school's relationship with parents has been dramatic – not least in that parents who would never have attended curriculum events now regularly spend time in their children's classrooms.

The teaching team at Rosendale further observed that there was a perception among adults and pupils that some children just 'knew how to learn', while others felt excluded from the learning process as they had labelled themselves as 'low ability' learners. Rosendale aims to overcome this through actively teaching metacognitive skills to children, which they then use during lessons. The children are taught that getting something wrong is a vital part of learning and that very few people are naturally 'good' at something – mostly they have become 'good' through lots and lots of practice. The false assumption that 'talent' does not require effort is discussed by authors such as Matthew Syed (2011), Malcolm Gladwell (2009), Gordon Stobart (2014), and particularly by Carol Dweck (1999, 2006, 2012). Challenging such assumptions – by providing constant examples within school of achievements throughout the community as a result of practice and skilled teaching – is not only an important way of validating such learning, but also provides the inspiration needed to continue to struggle when learning a new skill feels impossible.

The Wroxham Transformative Learning Alliance

Wroxham School was designated as a teaching school in 2011 and since that time a thriving alliance network of schools has developed. Learning forums (Rea et al. 2015) have been established for school leaders interested in debating research. Professional learning events have been developed by colleagues at Wroxham, enabling teachers from schools across the country and internationally to study in partnership. The ideas and practices of *Learning without Limits* (Hart et al. 2004) have attracted a great deal of interest and this, in tandem with the national reform of curriculum and assessment, has provided an opportunity for the Transformative Learning Alliance to support innovative, principled practice across England. The school, at the centre of the Alliance, has continued to develop and to maintain 'outstanding' achievement.

Through collaboration, sharing of ideas and a groundswell of opposition to labelling children (and schools), there is increasing momentum to reject punitive accountability in favour of peer review. This is not about a softening of so-called 'standards'; far from it, this is the opportunity needed for schools to break through the existing glass ceiling to achieve far more. The insights included in this book have been generously provided by school leaders and colleagues keen for an alternative voice to be heard. The voice of our Alliance is one of ambition to achieve greater opportunities for every child, within schools where teachers know they are trusted to build expertise in a dynamic culture of high expectations and innovation.

The Wroxham School: an update

Creating Learning without Limits told the story of how school improvement at Wroxham was informed by dispositions that enabled a climate of opportunity for all to flourish. The school continues to develop and to enable children to attain highly through inclusive pedagogy that refuses to label. Since publication of this book, Wroxham gained further recognition in 2013 with a third 'outstanding' judgement from Ofsted. In an Ofsted maths survey inspection in 2015, attainment at the school was celebrated:

> Pupils achieve exceptionally well in mathematics. From starting points on entry to the school that are broadly typical, pupils make good progress across the Early Years Foundation Stage and Key Stage 1. By the time they start Year 3, pupils are around one term above the national average. Progress across Key Stage 2 has been significantly above the national average for the past two years, as has attainment. At the end of Year 6, pupils are, on average, one year ahead of other pupils nationally.

> (See http://reports.ofsted.gov.uk)

I include this to provide further evidence that alternative approaches such as those based on *Learning without Limits* actually work. This book is not intended to be a celebration of Wroxham but aims to show what can happen when schools embrace the liberating idea that intelligence is not fixed. Once this has been realized, traditional classroom practices that behave as if every learner's future attainment is already pre-programmed become redundant.

I hope that the story of Wroxham and the many other schools included within this book instil confidence that enabling co-agency provides countless opportunities for children to surprise us. Miles, a 4-year-old who joined Wroxham having had a very difficult start in life, was featured in *Creating Learning without Limits*. Without the loving support of a new foster family and a school that refused to label him, Miles may not have succeeded. Indeed, I confess that when we received his test results in Year Six, confirming that he had achieved Level 5 in maths and English, I felt humbled by his achievements. Miles' story offers an irresistible example of what can happen when we resist notions of linearity and fixed 'ability'. He is now excelling in his secondary school and is a dedicated advocate for effort and hard work. When he left primary school he commented on his final report: *'I like Wroxham because it's creative and our learning is phenomenal.'* Miles' story is certainly 'phenomenal' and deserves to be noticed.

Conclusion

We have considered the impact that trust and co-agency has upon building the conditions necessary to think differently about issues such as 'ability', assessment and differentiation. We have seen how building a listening school enables us to 'find a way through' for every learner, rather than reverting to deficit notions of fixed capacity. Listening to the experiences of teachers and children in schools across England we have heard about how they are lifting limits by organizing their classrooms for genuinely inclusive practice that raises the expectations of everyone. Schools have shared their approaches to informing children and families about individual learning progress and leaders have shared ways in which they are building a culture of assessment that informs pedagogy rather than seeks to label teacher performance. Finally, we have heard stories of school improvement that transcend the all too common 'slash and burn' style of leadership, instead focusing on finding a better way for everyone to work together with high aspiration.

What we need next is to lead the way in finding a means to improve our accountability systems, informed and inspired by dispositions of trust, openness, generosity and professional courage. This may or may not be supported by policy-makers but, more importantly, as school leaders and teachers we have the opportunity (and responsibility) to make a difference for those within our own learning sphere today. We can make the decision to listen, to trust, to work collaboratively and most importantly, to believe that there *is* another way.

Bibliography

Alexander, R.J. (2008) *Towards Dialogic Teaching: Rethinking Classroom Talk* (4th edn). York: Dialogos.

Alexander, R.J. (ed.) (2010) *Children, their World, their Education: Final Report and Recommendations of the Cambridge Primary Review*. Oxford: Routledge.

Armstrong, M. (2006) *Children Writing Stories*. Maidenhead: Open University Press.

Black, P. and Wiliam, D. (1998) *Inside the Black Box: Raising Standards through Classroom Assessment*. London: GL Assessment.

Blasé, J. and Blasé, J. (2001) *Empowering Teachers: What Successful Principals Do*. Thousand Oaks, CA: Corwin Press.

Boaler, J. (2010) *The Elephant in the Classroom: Helping Children Learn and Love Maths*. London: Souvenir Press.

Boaler, J. (2013) *How to Learn Math* (video), https://class.stanford.edu/courses/Education/EDUC115N/How to Learn Math/about.

Boaler, J. (2016) *Mathematical Mindsets*. San Francisco, CA: Jossey-Bass.

Brooker, L. (2002) *Starting School – Young Children Learning Cultures*. Buckingham: Open University Press.

Browning, P. (2014) Why trust the head? Key practices for transformational school leaders to build a purposeful relationship of trust, *International Journal of Leadership in Education*, http://dx.doi.org/10.1080/13603124.2013.844275, retrieved 4 December 2014.

Bryk, A. and Schneider, B. (2002) *Trust in Schools: A Core Resource for Improvement*. New York: Russell Sage Foundation.

Bushe, G.R. (2012) Appreciative inquiry: theory and critique, in D. Boje, B. Burnes and J. Hassard (eds) *The Routledge Companion to Organizational Change*, pp. 87–103. Oxford: Routledge.

Clarke, S. (2014) *Outstanding Formative Assessment* London: Hodder Education.

Claxton, G. (2002) *Building Learning Power: Helping Young People Become Better Learners*. Bristol: TLO.

Claxton,G. and Lucas, B. (2015) *Educating Ruby*. Carmarthen: Crown House Publishing Ltd.

Corbett, P. and Strong, J. (2011) *Talk for Writing Across the Curriculum*. Maidenhead: Open University Press.

Dewey, J. (1934) *Art as Experience*. Carbondale, IL: Southern Illinois University Press, 1987.

DfE (Department for Education) (2013) *The National Curriculum in England: Framework for Key Stages 1 to 4*. London: DfE, www.gov.uk.

DfE (Department for Education) (2015) *Commission on Assessment Without Levels: Final Report*. London: DfE, www.gov.uk.

Dweck, C.S. (1999) *Self-theories: Their Role in Motivation, Personality and Development*. Philadelphia, PA: Psychology Press.

Dweck, C.S. (2006) *Mindset: The New Psychology of Success*. New York: Random House.

Dweck, C.S. (2012) *Mindset: How You Can Fulfill Your Potential*. New York: Ballantine Books.

Gilderdale, C. and Kiddle, A. (2011) *Adding and Subtraction Positive and Negative Numbers*, http://nrich.maths.org/5947.

Gladwell, M. (2009) *Outliers: The Story of Success*. London: Penguin Books.

Hart, S. (1998) A sorry tail: ability, pedagogy and educational reform, *British Journal of Educational Studies*, 46(2): 153–68.

Hart, S., Drummond, M.J., Dixon, A. and McIntyre, D. (2004) *Learning Without Limits*. Maidenhead: Open University Press.

Hattie, J. (2009) *Visible Learning*. London: Routledge.

Hattie, J. (2012) *Visible Learning for Teachers*. London: Routledge.

Lilly, J., Peacock, A., Shoveller, S. and Struthers, d'R. (2014) *Beyond Levels: Alternative Assessment Approaches Developed by Teaching Schools*, research report. London: National College for Teaching and Leadership.

Logue, C. (1969) *New Numbers*. London: Jonathan Cape.

Naylor, S., Keogh, B. and Goldsworthy, A. (2004) *Active Assessment Science*. Sandbach: Millgate House, www.millgatehouse.co.uk.

Peacock, A. (2011) *Circles of Influence*, in E. Sanders (ed.) *Leading a Creative School: Learning About Lasting School Change*. London: David Fulton.

Peacock, A. (2012) Developing outward-facing schools where citizenship is a lived experience, in J. Brown, H. Ross and P. Munn (eds) *Democratic Citizenship in Schools: Teaching Controversial Issues, Traditions and Accountability*. London: Dunedin Academic Press.

Phillipson, N. and Wegerif, R. (forthcoming) *Diologic Education: Mastering Core Concepts Through Thinking Together*. Abingdon: Taylor & Francis.

Price, A. (2010) *Amazing Adventures of Mr Wellington Boot!* London: Park Communications.

Rea, S., Sandals, L., Parish, N., Hill, R. and Gu, Q. (2015) *Leadership of Great Pedagogy in Teaching School Alliances: Research Case Studies*. London: National College for Teaching and Leadership.

Ricoeur, P. (2007) *From Text to Action*. Evanston, IL: Northwestern University Press.

Rowland, M. (2015) *An Updated Practical Guide to the Pupil Premium*. Woodbridge: John Catt.

Seleznyov, S. (2009) Giants, pixies and elves learning decimals, *Equals*, 15(1): 9–11.

Sotto, E. (1994) *When Teaching Becomes Learning: A Theory and Practice of Teaching*. London: Cassell.

Stobart, G. (2014) *The Expert Learner*. Maidenhead: McGraw-Hill Education.

Swann, M., Peacock, A., Hart, S. and Drummond, M.J. (2012) *Creating Learning without Limits*. Maidenhead: McGraw-Hill International.

Syed, M. (2011) *Bounce: The Myth of Talent and the Power of Practice*. London: Harper-Collins.

Taylor, C. (2013) The value of appreciative inquiry as an educational development tool, *Educational Developments*, 14(3): 23–6.

Tolstoy, L. (1982) *Tolstoy on Education*. London: Athlone Press.

Torrance, H. and Pryor, J. (2001) Developing formative assessment in the classroom: using action research to explore and modify theory, *British Educational Research Journal*, 27(5): 615–31.

von Glaserfeld, E. (1995) *Radical Constructivism: A Way of Knowing and Learning*. London: The Falmer Press.

von Goethe, J.W. (2006) *Theory of Colours*. New York: Dover Publications.

Vygotsky, L.S. (1962) *Thought and Language*. Cambridge, MA: Massachusetts Institute of Technology.

Webster, R., Russell, A. and Blatchford, P. (2015) *Maximising the Impact of Teaching Assistants: Guidance for School Leaders and Teachers*. Oxford: Routledge.

Wiliam, D. (2014) *Principled Assessment Design*. London: SSAT.

Index

ability grouping 18, 30, 44, 83, 86
  'choice and challenge' as alternative
    to 3, 51, 55, 57, 60, 62, 64, 117
  freedom from 83
  innovative leadership and
    alternative to 117–18
  liberation from, transformation and
    57–8
  organizational management and 59
    outstanding achievement without
      129–30
  pedagogy, alternative approaches
    to 3
  positive alternatives to,
    development of 51–2
  practice of (and alternatives to)
    51–2
  premises leading to 51–2
  rejection of labelling and 123–4
  whole-school approach to moving
    away from 62–3
accessibility to leadership 10
accountability measures 100
achievement and progress, articulation
  of 114–15
activity planning, colour-coded
  questions and 53–4
adventurous writing 55
affirmation, provision of 9
agency over choice of task,
  assessment of learning and 56–7

Alaalatoa, Barb 6
Alexander, Robin J. 7, 19, 34, 61
*Amazing Adventures of Mr Wellington
  Boot!* (Price, A.) 80–81
analysis of learning, children and 55
Anderson, Debbie 96–7
appreciation strategies, deployment
  of 9
argument, language of 45
Armstrong, Michael 64, 65, 70–80, 81
Art as Experience (Dewey, J.) 80
asking questions 42–3
aspiration, support for 128
assessment
  agency over choice of task,
    assessment of learning and
    56–7
  app for, development of 108–9
  assessment feedback, example of
    form of 112–13
  assessment for learning (AfL) 61–2
  Assessment Framework (NAHT,
    2014) 100–101
  Commission on Assessment without
    Levels 107
  as constant activity 53
  convergent and divergent
    assessment 39
  curriculum design, linking
    assessment to 109–10
  enhancement of 2

inclusive assessment practice 102–9
of learning, dialogue and 54
mindsets about, creation of change
    in 114–15
phonics and reading, assessment
    of 106
practice of, statements of 110–11
reporting to families, sharing
    assessment in 87–91
self-assessment
    encouragement of 23
    process of 53
    review and, process of 83, 85–6
summative assessment 52–3
whole-school assessment systems 3
see also dialogue, language for
    thinking and assessment through;
    reporting to families, sharing
    assessment in; whole-school
    approach to assessment; writing,
    assessment of
Atkins, Kate 129

Ban Khayang Pattana School, Thailand
    6–7
Banstead Infants School in Surrey
    54–5, 86
Barker, Sally 60–62
Beaudesert Lower School in Leighton
    Buzzard 26–8, 58–9
behaviour in school 48
Black, P. and Wiliam, D. 83
Blasé, J. and Blasé, J. 7
Boaler, Jo 38, 106
Bread Loaf School of English at
    Middlebury College, Vermont 70
Bridgewater Primary School in
    Northampton 23, 86, 116, 123–4
Brooker, L. 84
Browne, Anthony 80–81
Browning, Paul 4, 7, 8, 11
Bryk, Anthony 7, 9
Building Learning Power (Claxton,
    G.) 14
Burns, Kath 34–5, 116

Card, Lee 57
caring mode of thinking 19

Carlyle, Mark 62–3, 86–7
challenge
    'challenge approach,' introduction
        of 118–20
    challenge scale, example of 120
    challenge tasks, dealing with 54
    introduction of concept of 56
    see also 'choice and challenge'
characters in classes, delightful mixture
    of 52
Cherry Orchard School in
    Worcestershire 54, 57–8
Children, their World, their Education:
    final report of the Cambridge
    Primary Review (2010) 7
    dialogue, language for thinking and
        assessment 34
Children Writing Stories (Armstrong,
    M.) 70, 79
children's annual reports to families
    87–91
    child-teacher interactions, quality
        of 90–91
    feedback from parents 90–91
    report extracts 88–9, 89–90
    reports as evidence base 91
    whole school pro-forma for 88
children's voices, loss of interest in? 70
'choice and challenge' 3, 51, 55, 57, 60,
    62, 64, 117–18
Clarke, Shirley 106
class teaching, collaborative nature of
    61–2
Claxton, Guy 14–15, 54, 106
co-agency 23, 25, 33, 37, 61, 65, 87, 106,
    124, 131–2
    climate of trust and 6
    principle of 1, 3
    professional learning and 129
    teacher-learner co-agency 18
    whole-school approach to
        assessment 103
coaching of staff 10
cognitive conflict, dialogue inspired by
    40–41
collaborative mode of thinking 19
collective understanding, gauging of
    55

College Park Infants School in Portsmouth 96–7
'Come to the Edge' (Christopher Logue poem) 3
Commission on Assessment without Levels 107
communities of learners 35–6
comparison, language of 46
confidences, keeping of 11
connections in learning 5–6, 18–19, 36–7
Constantinou, Maria 92–3
consulting with students 114
convergent and divergent assessment 39
conversational engagement, opportunities for 19
Corbett, Pie 58
Coy, Lucy 117–18, 119, 120–21
Creating Learning without Limits (Swann et al. 2012) 1, 4, 6, 11, 18, 51–2, 103
    innovative leadership, transformability and 117, 119, 126, 129, 131–2
    reporting to families, sharing assessment in 84, 87
creative mode of thinking 19
creative writing, art of 70
critical mode of thinking 19
cross-moderation 100
cross-phase thinking 113–14
cultural capital building 128
curriculum breadth 2
curriculum content 111
curriculum creativity 3
curriculum design, linking assessment to 109–10
curriculum organization 36–7

data collection, positivity in use of 100
data dashboards 2
data sheets, avoidance of reliance on 52–3
Davey, Stephen 88–9
deadline setting 14
decision-making 8, 110
    consultative decision-making 10

deduction, language of 46
demeanor, consistency of 10
description, language of 46
descriptive writing 66
deterministic notions, unacceptability of 4
development work, staff involvement in 127
Dewey, John 80
dialogue
    assessment of learning and 54
    children and adults, impact of 19
    ideas and 18–19
    importance of 19
    purpose in, importance of 26
dialogue, language for thinking and assessment through 34–50
    argument, language of 45
    asking questions 42–3
    atmosphere of encouragement 48
    behaviour in school 48
    Children, their World, their Education: final report of the Cambridge Primary Review (2010) 34
    cognitive conflict, dialogue inspired by 40–41
    communities of learners 35–6
    comparison, language of 46
    connections in learning 36–7
    convergent and divergent assessment 39
    curriculum organization 36–7
    deduction, language of 46
    description, language of 46
    'dot talks,' idea of 38–9
    emotional safety 38
    evaluation, language of 46
    explanation, language of 46
    formative assessment 37
    hypothesis, language of 45
    joy of making language accessible 45–9
    knowledge sharing, preparedness for 43
    language accessibility 45–9
    language prompts 45–6
    language structures

Be The Best You Can Be (BTBYCB), aspiration and 48
collaborative writing 47
deployment of 45–9
learning choices 48
as tool for future fluency 47
mathematics 37–8
'Giant Palace, Let's Think' lesson 39–40
'Let's Think' programme 38–9
mathematical explanation, language of 46
robotic maths, avoidance of 41–2
memories, working with 34–5
non-judgementalism 37
numbers 38–9
opinion, language of 45
playtimes 49
prediction, language of 45
questioning answers 42–3
retelling, language of 45
sequencing, language of 46
Shakespeare, connecting with 43–5
summary 49–50
trust, importance of culture of 37
writing, structures for 49
differentiation in classroom practice 51
disengagement, dealing with 26–7
'dot talks,' idea of 38–9
Down's syndrome 91
Dweck, Carol S. 1–2, 56, 58, 106, 117, 123, 130

early intervention 102
Early Years Foundation Stage 19, 52, 61, 100, 108, 131
Easey, Nicky 89–90
East Barnet Secondary School 108
Eaton Primary School in Norfolk 116–17, 122
Education, Department for (DfE) 98, 100–101, 107
emotional safety 38
emotional well-being 23
empathetic listening 9
encouragement, atmosphere of 48
engagement with learning 53
English 'brain' (East Barnet School) 108

enrichment, support for 128
environmentally-friendly play spaces 21
evaluation
language of 46
of learning, 'habits of experts' and 54–5
every child's capacity to learn, focus on 4
everybody, principle of ethic of 1
excellence
pursuit of 97
recognition of? 112–15
experience, reflections on leadership
building momentum, gradual improvement and 15
disorganization 12–13
engagement with children 14–15
mistakes from first 11–12
trust lacking 13–14
turning point 15–16
expert learners
labelling, avoidance of 54–5
whole-school approach to assessment 106–8
explanation, language of 46

Facer, Tina 23–4, 34–5
'failure' of schools, label of 5–7
faith, values and '*sewa*' (service to others), all-through education rooted in 109–10
family consultations 84–5
feedback
to apprentice year six writers 65–9
assessment feedback, example of form of 112–13
to families 83
film in enhancement of 31
from lessons, importance of 32
from parents 90–91
scaffolding of learning through 55
see also formative feedback
Finch, Ed 96
Flintoff, Clare 45–7
formative assessment 37
self-evaluation through 106–7
formative feedback 83, 90

for children with additional needs 91–2
rigorous framework for 86
written formative feedback 103

getting to know what is needed to get better 94–5
Gilderdale, C. and Kiddle, A. 41
The Gingerbread Palace (Stanley, C.G.) 65
collaborative appraisal of 70–80
Gladwell, Malcolm 130
Goldsworthy, Anne 105
good teaching, art of 2
grades, negative impact of 83
Greenfield Academy in Bristol 86, 93, 94–5
growth mindset culture, reinforcement of 56

'hard to reach' parents, avoiding the label of 84
Hart, S., Drummond, M.J., Dixon, A. and McIntyre, D. 1, 4, 51–2, 106, 130
Hart, Susan 51–2
Harvey, Alison 23, 123–4
Hattie, J. 51, 105, 117
help stations in classrooms 119–20
'hot' and 'cold' tasks, implementation of 58
How to Learn Math (Boaler, J.) 38–9
Humphreys, Cathy 38
hypothesis, language of 45

ideas, sharing of 21
improvement and growth, key dispositions for 6
inclusion
inclusive assessment practice 102–9
inclusive maths mastery 60–62
liberating power of 3
positivity in 30–31
independence and understanding, support for 53
independent challenge tasks 54
independent working 53–4
individual progress, recording of 100
individual talk time 27

information for families 115
innovative leadership, transformability and 116–32
ability grouping, alternative to 117–18
aspiration, support for 128
'challenge approach,' introduction of 118–20
challenge scale, example of 120
'choice and challenge,' eradication of ability grouping with 117–18
cultural capital building 128
development work, staff involvement in 127
enrichment, support for 128
help stations in classrooms 119–20
institutional consistency, need for 124–5
learning, support for 128
listening to children 118
building trust and 126
metacognitive skills, active teaching of 130
moving from 'inadequate' to 'good' in less than a year 116–22
'no child slipping through the net,' culture of 123–4
outstanding achievement without 'ability' grouping 129–30
pedagogical skill, development of 128–9
pedagogy, avoidance of set limits in 122
positive default, leadership based on 127
positive learning behaviour, creation of 125–6
principled and courageous leadership, impacts of 116
rejection of ability grouping and labels at Bridgewater School 123–4
repertoire, development of 128–9
school day, structure of 130
self-differentiation, adaptation to 120–21
social capital building 128
staff, impacts on 120–21

staff actively supporting each other
126–7
summary 132
sustainable improvement 122
trust, transformative impact of 127
trust in teachers, placement of
124–9
whole-class teaching, cooperative
dynamism of 129–30
whole-school improvement 121–2
The Wroxham School, update on
progress at 131–2
The Wroxham Transformative
Learning Alliance 116, 130–32
institutional consistency, need for
124–5
interconnections 5–6
international concerns 2–3

knowledge sharing, preparedness for
43

labelling, avoidance of 51–64
ability grouping, practice of (and
alternatives to) 51–2
activity planning, colour-coded
questions and 53–4
adventurous writing 55
agency over choice of task,
assessment of learning and 56–7
analysis of learning, children and
55
assessment as constant activity 53
assessment of learning, dialogue
and 54
capacity to learn, limiting
assumptions about 51
challenge, introduction of concept
of 56
challenge tasks, dealing with 54
characters in classes, delightful
mixture of 52
class teaching, collaborative nature
of 61–2
collective understanding, gauging
of 55
data sheets, avoidance of reliance
on 52–3

dialogue, assessment of learning
and 54
differentiation in classroom practice
51
engagement with learning 53
evaluation of learning, 'habits of
experts' and 54–5
expert learners, children as 54–5
feedback, scaffolding of learning
through 55
growth mindset culture,
reinforcement of 56
'hot' and 'cold' tasks, implementation
of 58
inclusive maths mastery 60–62
independence and understanding,
support for 53
independent challenge tasks 54
independent working 53–4
learned helplessness 51
learning activities, offer of choice
of 53–4
learning capacity, building of 53
learning habits, selection of 54–5
learning partners, pair working and
59–60
learning process, children as
partners in 54–5
listening to children matters 52
marking children's work 53
maths formats, use of variation of
62
misconceptions, teaching
opportunities within 61
openness, disposition of 52
peer learning 58–9
planning and preparing lessons
52–3, 53–4
prior attainment grids, avoidance of
reliance on 52–3
progress, trust and 'choice and
challenge' 55–7
self-assessment, process of 53
summary 64
summative assessment 52–3
tasks, choices of 52
thinking, development of skills that
explain 55

transformation of year five 57–8
  growth, interest in idea of 58
  strategies implemented in 57–8
whole-school approach 62–4
language accessibility 45–9
language prompts 45–6
language structures
  Be The Best You Can Be (BTBYCB),
    aspiration and 48
  collaborative writing 47
  deployment of 45–9
  learning choices 48
  as tool for future fluency 47
Larkrise Primary in Oxfordshire 95–6
leadership
  accessibility to 10
  assessment and 16–17
  core ideas of 3
  leadership theory, reality and 11–16
  need for clarity in 13
  practices of, building trust through
    8–11
  see also experience, reflections on
    leadership
league tables 2
learned helplessness 51
learning
  'can-do' learning 27–8
  capacity for, building of 53
  capacity for, limiting assumptions
    about 51
  communities of learners 35–6
  connections in 5–6, 18–19, 36–7
  in culture of trust 4
  engagement with 53
  evaluation of, 'habits of experts' and
    54–5
  habits of, selection of 54–5
  learning activities, offer of choice
    of 53–4
  learning conferences 86
  learning council (Moss Hey School)
    24–5
  learning journals 102–3
  learning review meetings 85–7
  measurability of 2
  pair working and partners 59–60
  partnership in, working with 103

performance of, assessment of
    100–102
process of, children as partners in
    54–5
self-awareness of children's own
    learning , building up 86–7
support for, innovative leadership
    and 128
targets for, self-generation of 94
Learning without Limits (Hart et al.
    2004) 1, 2–3, 4, 26, 45, 65, 84, 95,
    106
innovative leadership,
    transformability and 117, 130,
    131
labelling, avoidance of 51, 52, 57, 60
leading for 7–8
principles and ideas of, momentum
    for 4–5
Lilly, J., Peacock, A., Shoveller, S. and
    Struthers, d'R. 92–3
limit setting, refusal of 3
listening actively 9
listening ethos, building whole-school
    structures in support of 18
listening to children, importance of
    18–33, 52
  'can-do' learning 27–8
  caring mode of thinking 19
  co-agency between teacher and
    learners 18
  collaborative mode of thinking 19
  connections in learning, importance
    of 18–19
  conversational engagement,
    opportunities for 19
  creative mode of thinking 19
  critical mode of thinking 19
  dialogue
    children and adults, impact of 19
    ideas and 18–19
    importance of 19
    purpose in, importance of 26
  disengagement, dealing with 26–7
  emotional well-being 23
  environmentally-friendly play
    spaces 21
  feedback

film in enhancement of 31
from lessons, importance of 32
finding a voice 31
ideas, sharing of 21
inclusion, positivity in 30–31
individual talk time 27
learning council (Moss Hey School) 24–5
listening ethos, building whole-school structures in support of 18
listening to children 23–5
listening to those who find learning difficult 26–9
mathematics, confidence in 27
mixed-age circle meetings 20–21
organizational structures that facilitate listening 20–21
pedagogy, impact on 32
peer mediation 21–3
'rights respecting' ethos 25–6
self-assessment, encouragement of 23
spoken word, importance of 19
subject-specific vocabulary 19
summary 32–3
thinking, modes of (and harmony between) 19
topic books 25
transition to secondary school 29–31
trust
    building culture of 18
    development and earning of 28–9
whole-school forum (Park Street) 23–4
whole-school maths meeting 27
listening to children, innovative leadership and 118
building trust 126
Logue, Christopher 3
Lucas, Bill 106

Macdonald, Alasdair 124–5, 128
McSorley, Ela 99, 109–10, 111, 112
Mae Fa Luang Foundation 6–7
marking children's work 53
Mathematical Mindsets (Boaler, J.) 38

mathematics 37–8
confidence in 27
formats in, use of variation of 62
'Giant Palace, Let's Think' lesson 39–40
inclusive maths mastery 60–62
'Let's Think' programme 38–9
mathematical explanation, language of 46
robotic maths, avoidance of 41–2
whole-school maths meeting 27
memories, working with 34–5
Mence, Cheryl 104
mentoring of staff 10
Meredith Infant School in Portsmouth 31, 84–5
metacognitive skills, active teaching of 130
metaphor, introduction of idea of 67
A Midsummer Night's Dream (Shakespeare, W.) 44
mindsets about assessment, creation of change in 114–15
misconceptions, teaching opportunities within 61
mistakes, admission of 8–9
mixed-age circle meetings 20–21
monitoring progress at The Wroxham School 99–100
Monti, Vittorio 36
morale, trust and 6
Morpeth Secondary School in London 116, 124–5, 127, 128–9
Moss Hey School in Stockport 34–5

National Association of Headteachers (NAHT) 100–101
National Curriculum 2, 87, 98
assessment, whole-school approach to 99–100, 101, 102, 106–7, 109, 114
Naylor, S., Keogh, B. and Goldsworthy, A. 105
Nishkam High School in Birmingham 99, 109–15
'no child slipping through the net,' culture of 123–4
non-judgementalism 37

NRich teacher guides 41
numbers 38–9

Ollerton, Mike 42–3
Open Futures 36–7
openness, disposition of 52
opinion, language of 45
opportunity, culture of 3
optimism fuelled by involvement, need
    for 5
organizational performance and trust 7
organizational structures that facilitate
    listening 20–21
Osfted 12, 15, 16, 99, 102, 103–4
    innovative leadership,
        transformability and 116–17, 124,
        127, 131
outstanding achievement without
    'ability' grouping 129–30

parents as child's first teacher, principle
    of 84
Park Street School in Hertfordshire
    23–4, 25, 34–5
Peacock, A. 21
Pearce, Vanessa 26–8, 58–9
Peckham, Sharon 31, 84–5
pedagogy
    avoidance of set limits in 122
    development of skill in 128–9
    listening to children, impact on 32
pedagogy, alternative approaches to
    1–2
    'ability,' downsides of idea of 2
    ability grouping, alternative to 3
    assessment, enhancement of 2
    'Come to the Edge' (Christopher
        Logue poem) 3
    curriculum breadth 2
    curriculum creativity 3
    data dashboards 2
    good teaching, art of 2
    inclusion, liberating power of 3
    international concerns 2–3
    leadership, core ideas of 3
    league tables 2
    learning, measurability of 2
    limit setting, refusal of 3

opportunity, culture of 3
performance, domination of 2
'personal best,' trust and seeking
    for 2
quality of teaching 2
tests and exams, over-domination
    of 2
transformative leadership 3
voices, structures for hearing 3
whole-school assessment systems 3
Wroxham School, system of choice
    and challenge at 3
peer learning 58–9
peer mediation 21–3
performance
    culture of trust and 7–8
    domination of 2
    performance management 103–4
'personal best,' trust and seeking for 2
personnel issues 14
Phillipson, N. and Wegerif, R. 19
phonics and reading, assessment of
    106
planning and preparing lessons 52–3,
    53–4
playtimes 49
poetic use of language 66–9
positive default, leadership based on
    127
positive learning behaviour, creation
    of 125–6
prediction, language of 45
presentations, listening to 87
Price, Ashley 80–81
prior attainment grids, avoidance of
    reliance on 52–3
professional learning 96–7
progress, trust and 'choice and
    challenge' 55–7
progress meetings 104–5
publishing young author's work 80–81
pupil passports 92–3

quality of teaching
    pedagogy, alternative approaches
        to 2
    whole-school approach to
        assessment 103–4

Queensland University of Technology 7
questioning answers 42–3

Rea, S., Sandals, L., Parish, N., Hill, R.
    and Gu, Q. 130
reading, assessment of 105–6
record-keeping grid, example of 101
Reilly, Jemima 124–5
relationships, establishment of 13
repertoire, development of 128–9
reporting to families, sharing
        assessment in 83–98
    ability grouping, freedom from 83
    children's annual reports to families
        87–91
        child-teacher interactions, quality
            of 90–91
        feedback from parents 90–91
        report extracts 88–9, 89–90
        reports as evidence base 91
        whole school pro-forma for 88
    excellence, pursuit of 97
    family consultations 84–5
    feedback
        to families 83
        from parents 90–91
    formative feedback 83, 90
        for children with additional needs
            91–2
        rigorous framework for 86
        written formative feedback 103
    getting to know what is needed to
        get better 94–5
    grades, negative impact of 83
    'hard to reach' parents, avoiding the
        label of 84
    learning conferences 86
    learning review meetings 85–7
    learning targets, self-generation of
        94
    parents as child's first teacher,
        principle of 84
    PowerPoint presentations 87
    presentations, listening to 87
    professional learning 96–7
    pupil passports 92–3
    self-assessment and review, process
        of 83, 85–6
        astuteness in 96

    gaining insights from 85–6
    self-awareness of children's own
        learning , building up 86–7
    summary 98
    summative reports, breaking with
        tradition on 93–6
    thinking, articulation of 83
    trust and openness, culture of 83
    video presentations 84–5
    web-based application 95–6
retelling, language of 45
Richards, Ann 26
Richardson, Kate 86, 93–4
Ricoeur, Paul 77
'rights respecting' ethos 25–6
Rolls, Luke 32, 37–8, 38–9, 39–40, 41–2,
    59–60
Rosendale Primary School in London
    116, 129–30
Rowland, M. 51

SATs tests 34, 35, 116, 121
Schneider, Barbara 7, 9
school day, structure of 130
Scole School in Norfolk 54, 62–3, 96–7
Seleznyov, S. 39
self-assessment
    encouragement of 23
    process of 53
    review and, process of 83, 85–6
        astuteness in 96
        gaining insights from 85–6
self-awareness of children's own
        learning , building up 86–7
self-differentiation, adaptation to
    120–21
self-editing 69
sequencing, language of 46
Shakespeare, connecting with 43–5
Smith, Tabitha 24–5
social capital building 128
social construction of trust 8
Sotto, E. 43
spoken word, importance of 19
St Helen's School in Ipswich 45–9
St Mary's School in Barnet 92–3
St Nicolas Junior School in West
    Berkshire 34–5, 116

Stanley, Ceva Gabrielle 71–9
Stobart, Gordon 130
Storrar, Stephanie 55, 106–7
Strong, Julia 58
subject knowledge
    appropriate use of 68
    development of 105
subject mastery, notions of 111–12
subject-specific vocabulary 19
successful teaching, evidence of 103–4
summaries
    dialogue, language for thinking and
        assessment through 49–50
    innovative leadership,
        transformability and 132
    labelling, avoidance of 64
    listening to children, importance of
        32–3
    reporting to families, sharing
        assessment in 98
    trust, building professional learning
        culture of 17
    whole-school approach to
        assessment 115
    writing, assessment of 81–2
summative assessment 52–3
summative reports, breaking with
        tradition on 93–6
Sunnyfields in Barnet 26, 96
sustainable improvement 122
Swann, M., Peacock, A., Hart, S. and
        Drummond, M.J. 1, 4, 18, 51–2,
        117, 126
Swiss Cottage Special School in London
        92–3
Syed, Matthew 130
Sylvia Park School in Auckland 6

tasks, choices of 52
tests and exams, over-domination of 2
Theory of Colours (Von Goethe, J.W.)
        79
thinking
    articulation of 83
    development of skills that explain
        55
    modes of (and harmony between)
        19

Thomas, Norman 36
Thomas, Rebecca 57, 58
Tolstoy, Leo 77
topic books 25
Torrance, H. and Pryor, J. 39
Torres, Fernando 47
Tower Hamlets EMA Team in London
        45
tracking windscreen, example of 107
transformation of year five 57–8
    growth, interest in idea of 58
    strategies implemented in 57–8
transformative leadership 3
transition to secondary school 29–31
trust
    building culture of 18
    development and earning of 28–9
    importance of culture of 37
    openness and, culture of 83
    principle of 1, 2, 3, 4
    progress meetings and 104–5
    in teachers, placement of 124–9
    transformative impact of 127
trust, building professional learning
        culture of 4–17
    accessibility to leadership 10
    affirmation, provision of 9
    appreciation strategies, deployment
        of 9
    building trust 7
    co-agency, climate of trust and 6
    coaching of staff 10
    confidences, keeping of 11
    consistency of demeanor 10
    consultative decision-making 10
    deadline setting 14
    deterministic notions,
        unacceptability of 4
    empathetic listening 9
    every child's capacity to learn, focus
        on 4
    experience, reflections on leadership
        building momentum, gradual
            improvement and 15
        disorganization 12–13
        engagement with children 14–15
        mistakes from first 11–12
        trust lacking 13–14

turning point 15–16
'failure' of schools, label of 5–7
improvement and growth, key
	dispositions for 6
interconnections 5–6
leadership
	assessment and 16–17
	need for clarity in 13
	practices of, building trust through
		8–11
leadership theory, reality and 11–16
leading for *Learning without Limits*
	7–8
learning in culture of trust 4
listening actively 9
mentoring of staff 10
mistakes, admission of 8–9
morale 6
optimism fuelled by involvement,
	need for 5
organizational performance and
	trust 7
performance, culture of trust and
	7–8
personnel issues 14
relationships, establishment of 13
social construction of trust 8
summary 17
trust, key principle of 4
trust, offering of 9
visibility 10

UN Convention on the Rights of the
	Child (1989) 26
UNICEF UK 25–6
University of Cambridge Primary
	School 32, 37, 59–60

video presentations 84–5
visibility, trust and 10
voices
	children's voices, loss of interest
		in? 70
	finding a voice 31
	structures for hearing 3
von Glasersfeld, E. 43
Von Goethe, J.W. 79
Vygotsky, L.S. 130

Webster, R., Russell, A. and Blatchford,
	P. 51
whole-class teaching, cooperative
	dynamism of 129–30
whole-school approach, avoidance of
	labelling and 62–4
whole-school approach to assessment
	99–115
	accountability measures 100
	achievement and progress,
		articulation of 114–15
	assessment app, development of
		108–9
	assessment feedback, example of
		form of 112–13
	Assessment Framework (NAHT,
		2014) 100–101
	assessment practice, statements of
		110–11
	co-agency 103
	Commission on Assessment without
		Levels 107
	consulting with students 114
	cross-moderation 100
	cross-phase thinking 113–14
	curriculum content 111
	curriculum design, linking
		assessment to 109–10
	data collection, positivity in use of
		100
	early intervention 102
	English 'brain' (East Barnet School)
		108
	excellence, recognition of? 112–15
	expert learners 106–8
	faith, values and '*sewa*' (service to
		others), all-through education
		rooted in 109–10
	formative assessment, self-
		evaluation through 106–7
	inclusive assessment practice 102–9
	individual progress, recording of
		100
	information for families 115
	learning journals 102–3
	learning partner, working with 103
	learning performance, assessment of
		100–102

mindsets about assessment, creation
of change in 114–15
monitoring progress at The
Wroxham School 99–100
performance management 103–4
phonics and reading, assessment
of 106
principles for guiding assessment
110
progress meetings 104–5
quality of teaching 103–4
reading, assessment of 105–6
record-keeping grid, example of 101
subject knowledge, development of
105
subject mastery, notions of 111–12
successful teaching, evidence of
103–4
summary 115
tracking windscreen, example of
107
trust underlying progress meetings
104–5
written formative feedback 103
whole-school assessment systems 3
whole-school forum (Park Street) 23–4
whole-school improvement 121–2
whole-school maths meeting 27
Wiliam, D. 83
Worsley, Laura 124–5
writing, assessment of 65–82
  *Amazing Adventures of Mr
  Wellington Boot*! (Price, A.) 80–81
  Art as Experience (Dewey, J.) 80
  assessing writing 65
  Children Writing Stories
  (Armstrong, M.) 70, 79
  children's voices, loss of interest
  in? 70
  creative writing, art of 70

descriptive writing 66
feedback to apprentice year six
writers 65–9
The Gingerbread Palace (Stanley,
C.G.) 65
  collaborative appraisal of 70–80
  metaphor, introduction of idea of
  67
  poetic use of language 66–9
  publishing young author's work
  80–81
  self-editing 69
  subject knowledge, appropriate use
  of 68
  summary 81–2
  Theory of Colours (Von Goethe,
  J.W.) 79
writing, structures for 49
written formative feedback 103
Wroxham Friends Association 21
The Wroxham School 1, 5–6, 11, 65, 69,
80
  dialogue, assessment through 35,
  36, 39, 43
  innovative leadership,
  transformability and 116, 117,
  130–32
  labelling, avoidance of 51–2, 59, 60
  listening to children, importance of
  19, 20–21, 28, 29–30
  monitoring progress at 99–100
  reporting to families 84, 85, 87, 91,
  94
  system of choice and challenge at 3
  update on progress at 131–2
  whole-school approach to
  assessment 99–100, 102, 103–4,
  105
The Wroxham Transformative Learning
Alliance 116, 130–32

LEARNING WITHOUT LIMITS

Susan Hart, Annabelle Dixon, Mary Jane
Drummond & Donald McIntyre

ISBN: 9780335212590 (Paperback)
eBook: 9780335262519
2004

This book explores ways of teaching that are free from determinist beliefs
about ability. In a detailed critique of the practices of ability labelling and
ability-focussed teaching, *Learning without Limits* examines the damage
these practices can do to young people, teachers and the curriculum.

Drawing on a research project at the University of Cambridge, the book
features nine vivid case studies (from Year 1 to Year 11) that describe how
teachers have developed alternative practices despite considerable pressure
on them and on their schools and classrooms.

www.mheducation.co.uk

CREATING LEARNING WITHOUT LIMITS

Mandy Swann, Alison Peacock, Susan Hart and
Mary Jane Drummond

ISBN: 9780335242115 (Paperback)
eBook: 9780335242139

2012

This book tells the story of what one primary school community learned
about how to create education based on inclusive, egalitarian principles, in
an environment free from determinist beliefs about ability. Their collective
work was guided by the findings of a previous project, Learning Without
Limits (Hart, Dixon, Drummond and McIntyre, 2004), an empirical study of
nine individual teachers who had rejected the concept of fixed ability. The
authors explored what these teachers found themselves able to do, in their
own classrooms, to increase the capacity to learn of all children and young
people.

Key features:

- Presents empirical evidence of strategies and practices that the staff
  group used in the development of a whole school approach
- Key ideas and findings are presented through vivid personal accounts
  of individual teachers' and the head teacher's practice
- Chapters including vignettes of classroom life, drawing on
  observations and interviews

www.mheducation.co.uk

OPEN UNIVERSITY PRESS
McGraw - Hill Education